C O N T E M P O R A R Y A R T

FROM CRESCENT MOON PUBLISHING

JASPER JOHNS

JASPER JOHNS

L.M. Poole

Crescent Moon

Crescent Moon Publishing
P.O. Box 393
Maidstone
Kent
ME14 5XU, U.K.

First published 1994. Fourth edition 2011.
© L.M. Poole 2011.

Printed and bound in the U.S.A.
Set in Rotis SemiSans 10 on 15pt.
Designed by Radiance Graphics.

British Library Cataloguing in Publication data

Poole, L.M.
Jasper Johns
I. Title
759.13

ISBN-13 9781861712905

CONTENTS

ACKNOWLEDGEMENTS

To the authors and publishers quoted.
To the copyright holders of the illustrations.
Every effort has been made to contact the copyright holders of the illustrations. Enquiries are welcomed for future editions of this book.

B. – The situation is that of him who is helpless, cannot act, in the event cannot paint, since he is obliged to paint. The act is of him who, helpless, unable to act, acts, in the event paints, since he is obliged to paint.

D. – Why is he obliged to paint?

B. – I don't know.

D. – Why is he helpless to paint?

B. – Because there is nothing to paint and nothing to paint with.

Samuel Beckett, *Three Dialogues*, with Géorges Dutuit

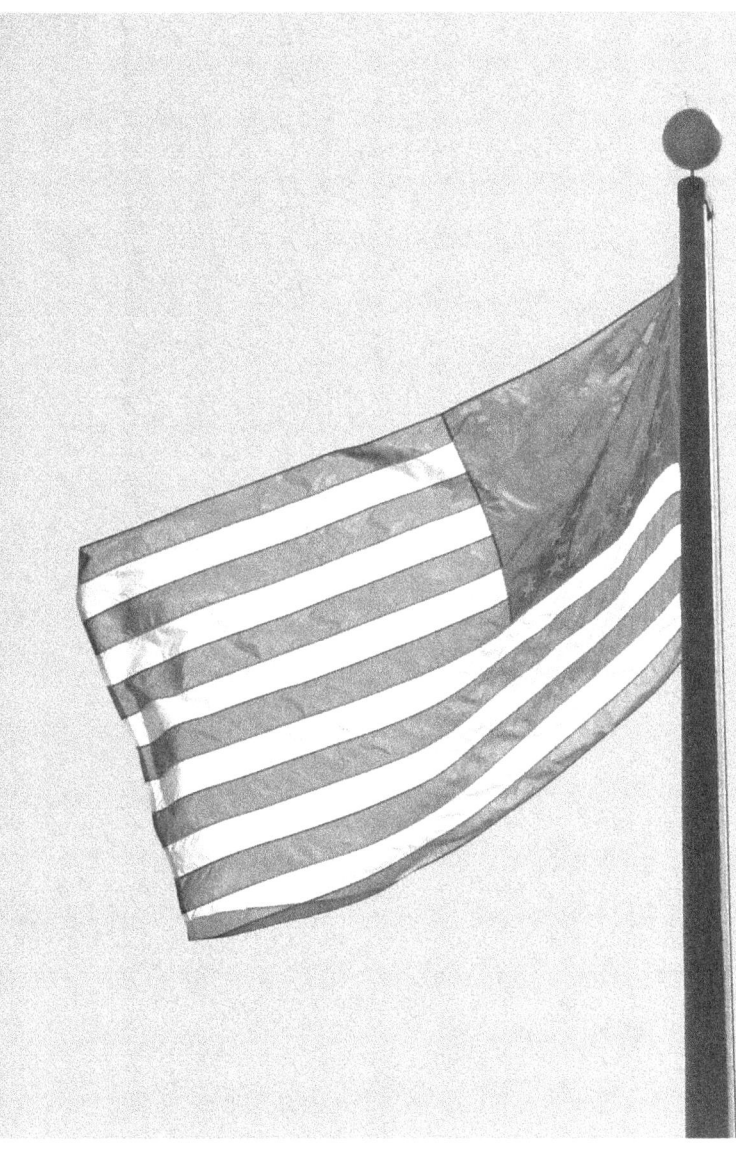

The U.S. flag, the basis for some of Jasper Johns' most celebrated works.

Jasper Johns explained:

Using the design of the American flag took care of a great deal for me because I didn't have to design it. So I went on to similar things like the targets – things the mind already knows. That gave me room to work on other levels.

1 : THE SENSUALITY OF SURFACES

The problem is not doing something, the problem is knowing what one wants to do.

Jasper Johns[1]

American artist Jasper Johns was born in 1930 in Augusta, Georgia, and grew up in Allendale, South Carolina.[2] He moved to New York City in 1949, where he remained for much of his life (more recently he has lived in Connecticut). Johns was associated with artists such as Marcel Duchamp, one of his heroes, and Robert Rauschenberg, with whom he lived in 1950s. His first solo show was in 1958 (at Leo Castelli in Gotham). Johns has become one of the U.S.A.'s premier artists, guaranteed a mention in *any* critical study or art history book of modern art and contemporary art, American art, and *avant garde* art.[3]

---

1 J. Johns, quoted in Daniel Wheeler, 139

2 'In the place where I was a child, there were no artists and there was no art, so I really didn't know what that meant. I think I thought it meant that I would be in a situation different than the one that I was in.'

3 Jasper Johns has even appeared in America's finest comedy show, *The Simpsons*, in an episode where Homer becomes an 'outsider' artist, and Johns steals lightbulbs.

Among the key shows of Jasper Johns are: Stedelijk Museum, Amsterdam (1972), Krefeld (1976), Frankfurt (1986), New York's MOMA (1996, 2007, 2009), the Whitney (1996), Basel (1997), Cologne (1997, 2001), San Francisco's MOMA (1999), Washington, DC (2001), a travelling show, visiting Minneapolis, Edinburgh, Valencia, South Carolina and Dublin (2003), L.A. (2004), Amarillo (2005), Chicago and the Met (2007). In the 2000s travelling shows of prints and drawings have appeared in many cities around the world.

Jasper Johns' reputation was greatly enhanced in the late Eighties by the boom in the economics of the art world: on November 9, 1988, Johns' *White Flag* fetched $7 million in a sale of the Burton and Emily Tremaine collection. Johns' *False Start* went for $17 million the following day, from Victor W. Ganz's collection. These were huge prices for a living artist.[4]

The works of Jasper Johns are certainly among the most sensual of all contemporary artists' works – in his manipulation of paint and texture and surface: Johns does not depict naked women or the usual trappings of erotic art. In fact, there are no naked women or men in his art. Bits of bodies, yes – a handprint, the cast of a leg, masks, critics' mouths – but not the usual sex objects of Western art. (Although Johns did make an image of his own 'genitalia and buttocks' in 1973's *Skin I* and *Skin II*.)[5]

Instead, the eroticism of Jasper Johns' works comes from his incredible surfaces, which are made of oil and wax (or encaustic), spread thickly on the canvas. Paintings such as *White Flag* (1955) , *Highway,* (1959), *Canvas* (1956), and *Scent* (1973-74) are really exquisite works, so intensely tactile

---

4 I. Sandler, 1996, 519.

5 J. Johns: *Skin I,* 1973, charcoal on paper, 25.5 x 40.25in, collection: the artist; *Skin II*, 1973, charcoal on paper, 25.5 x 40.25in, collection: the artist. See M. Rosenthal, 18

and sumptuous.[6] Johns' drawings with ink are just as sumptuous – ink is drawn onto plastic, so the colours swirl and merge into each other, in effects akin to marbling.[7]

The sensuality of surfaces, of textures, of brushwork, of the artist's sense of touch, is crucial to the 'greatness' of art, as Lynda Nead writes:

> the artist's subjectivity that is registered by the brushwork and surface is sexualized. Art criticism writes sex into descriptions of paint, surface and forms. (58)

Paul Gauguin wrote of the sensual primacy of painting in the familiar terms of late 19th century Baudelairean 'theory of correspondences' which was used by many poets, painters and dramatists:

> Painting is the most beautiful of all arts. In it, all sensations are condensed... A complete art which sums up all the others and completes them. – Like music, it acts on the soul through the intermediary senses: harmonious colours correspond to the harmonies of sounds.[8]

Frank Stella, one of the key contemporaries of Jasper Johns, writes of the space a painting creates,[9] and how this space can envelop the viewer, sensually:

---

6 *White Flag*, 1955, encaustic and collage on canvas, 78 x 120.8in, collection: the artist; *Highway*, 1959, encaustic and collage on canvas, 190.5 x 154.9cm, collection: Mrs Leo Castelli, New York, NY; *Scent*, 1973-4, oil and encaustic on canvas, 182.9 x 320.6cm, collection: Ludwig Aachen; *Canvas*, 1956, encaustic and collage on canvas with objects, 76.2 x 63.5cm, collection; the artist. See R. Bernstein, 1985; R. Francis, 1984; M. Kozloff, 1969.

7 J. Johns: *Untitled*, 1983, ink on plastic, 24.8 x 36.2in, Museum of Modern Art, New York, NY; *Perilous Night*, 1982, ink on plastic, 31.6 x 40.8in, collection: the artist; *Untitled*, 1983-4, ink on plastic, 26.2 x 34.5in, collection: the artist

8 P. Gauguin: "Notes Synthetiques", in *Paul Gauguin: A Sketchbook*, tr Raymond Cogniat, Hammer Galleries, New York, NY, 1962, 57f

9 Jasper Johns has said: 'Most of the power of painting comes through the manipulation of space... but I don't understand that.'

An effective painting should present its space in such a way as to include both viewer and maker each with his own space intact. It is not that this experience should be literal; it is simply that the sense of space projected by the painting should seem expansive: expansive enough to include the viewing and the creation of that space. (*Working Space*, 9)

Jasper Johns remarked: 'I think a painting should include more experience than simply intended statement.' Other artists have spoken lovingly of the loving nature of the canvas itself, the beauty of the art object. Maurice Denis wrote: '[t]he emotion – bitter or sweet, "literary" as the painters say – emerges from the canvas itself, a plane surface covered with colours.'[10]

Jasper Johns was relatively successful early on in his career, as with his contemporaries Frank Stella and Robert Rauschenberg. Some people might point out that Johns wasn't really successful in his youth – but he was, compared to the thousands and millions of artists around the world who were making art with little or no recognition whatsoever (and it's the same today – only a tiny fraction receive glory – or even modest success). Peter Fuller wrote:

In 1958, Alfred Barr cooled his support of Abstract Expressionism, and urged artists to rebel against their elders. Significantly, Barr, too, was involved in the manufacture of Jasper Johns. Until 1958, Johns was an obscure artist who had inserted certain Dada-esque representational components into what was essentially a modified Abstract Expressionist style. That year, he was given a one-man show by Castelli; before it opened, the decision had been taken to put him on the front cover of *Art News* (hitherto a partisan Abstract Expressionist publication). MOMA immediately purchased examples of his work.[11]

In that important year, 1958, Stella was 22 and Johns was 28.

---

10 Maurice Denis: "Definitions of neotraditionism", 1890, in *Theories: 1890-1910*, Rouart et Watelin, Paris 1920, 5f

11 Peter Fuller: "American Painting Since Last Year", *Art Monthly*, June 1979, in David Shapiro, 178

2 : OIL AND WAX

One works without thinking how to work.

Jasper Johns

A sense of space is crucial for Jasper Johns.[12] 'As well as I can tell,' he says, 'I am concerned with space. With some idea about space. And then as soon as you break space, then you have things'.[13]

Jasper Johns works very closely with his paintings, becoming absorbed totally in the surfaces, as a his friend Michael Crichton wrote:

> when he is working, Jasper is totally concentrated on those surfaces. He lives in those surfaces. The surfaces are his whole world, they are everything. He loses himself in them. They are everything'.[14]

Jasper Johns works intuitively, instinctively: 'One works without thinking how to work,' he has said. And: 'I have no ideas about what the paintings

----

12 'One likes to think that one anticipates changes in the spaces we inhabit, and our ideas about space.'

13 Quoted in P. Fuller, 1978, 12.

14 Quoted in M. Crichton, 1977, 21.

imply about the world. I don't think that's a painter's business. He just paints paintings without a conscious reason.' Johns has faith in the power of the unconscious: it would work out what needed to be done: 'The thing is, if you believe in the unconscious - and I do - there's room for all kinds of possibilities that I don't know how you prove one way or another.'

Jasper Johns' tactile surfaces are built up using wax – the thick impasto of oil and wax is one of the keys to his textures, for when the wax cools, you can paint on top of it very soon, instead of waiting for the paint to dry (in ib., 28). Johns' used encaustic and oil because he wanted evidence of the gestures he made *before* and *after*, that is, a finished painting which would reveal its making.

You can look at just a segment of a Jasper Johns painting on a wall in a museum, and you know it's by Johns. His surfaces are very distinctive – there are no other painters quite like him around.

Jasper Johns said:

> It was very simple. I wanted to show what had gone before in a picture, and what was done after. But if you put on a heavy brushstroke in paint, and then add another stroke, the second smears the first under the paint unless the paint is dry. And paint takes too long to dry. I didn't know what to do. Then someone suggested wax. It worked very well as soon as the wax was cool I could put on another stroke, and it would not alter the first.[15]

These are the seemingly simple and obvious techniques and stratagems that concern artists, this dealing with such simple but important processes such as drying paint. Artists are, typically, humble, and Johns here says it 'was very simple', yet it is also crucial.

Marcel Duchamp and Kurt Schwitters are usually cited as precursors of Jasper Johns' mixed media explorations. Duchamp is cited regularly in Johns criticism, and was one of his major influences artistically. Other influences include John Cage and Merce Cunningham.

Robert Rauschenberg and Jasper Johns rewrote the notion of painting-as-object by sticking objects onto it. Kurt Schwitters is often cited as a

---

15 Quoted in D. Wheeler, 134-5.

major exponent of multi-media formalism. Schwitters explained how he
came to do it:

> I simply could not see any reason why old streetcar tickets, driftwood, coat
> checks, wire and wheel parts, buttons, junk from the attic and heaps of refuse
> should not be used as material for paintings, any less than colours made in a
> factory.[16]

For Jasper Johns, the use of objects and quotes became modernist and
ironic. Before Roy Lichtenstein had aped the Abstract Expressionists, writes
David Anfam, Johns been making ironic art-about-art statements:

> Well beforehand, however, Johns had multiplied such ironic displacements and
> his *Field Painting* (1963-64) condenses a decade of them. Item by item, ideals
> from the past generation are processed into alien disguises: their symbolic
> chiaroscuro calls forth a light switch in a darkly painted passage (above left of
> centre), the encounter with materials yields several pots and brushes, lettering
> replaces noumenal chroma and depth gapes through a central break, the
> passive antitype of Newman's heroically virile 'zip'. Literary parallels to this
> replacement of a humanized vision by one of mirrored textual codes and
> signifiers were William Gaddis's novel *The Recognitions* (1955) and the overall
> drift into post-modernity announced in the fictions of John Barth and Thomas
> Pynchon (*V,* 1963). (202-3)

This form of self-reflexive, *mise-en-â byme* commentary is so familiar
to us now. It's found not only in the postmodern literature of the 1950s
and 1960s, but also in the fiction of, say, André Gide. Gide's 1926 novel
The Counterfeiters is a key text in this respect: the main character
(Edouard) is, of course, a novelist. But Edouard is more interested not in the
novel he's trying to write, but in his book about the writing of his novel.
Thus, the diary/ journal as an object becomes more important than the
artwork itself; and the act of *writing about* the art becomes more
important than *making* the artwork itself.

Indeed, so crucial was the making of the book *The Counterfeiters* to
André Gide that he published a book after *The Counterfeiters,* called
precisely that, *The Journal of The Counterfeitiers* (although he swore he'd

---

16 Quoted in F. Roh, 133.

never do that – despising artists 'explaining' their works). Much of Gide's concerns are also those of Jasper Johns. For, like the readymades of Marcel Duchamp, Gide's *The Counterfeiters* destroys the diegetic effect of fiction, its naturalism and believability. Like Jean-Luc Godard's movies and Jasper Johns' paintings, Gide's novel is self-reflexive art, a Pop Art novel forty years before Pop Art (Godard's cinema of the 1960s is pure Pop Art, comicbook movies in red, blue, white and yellow, like Johns or Roy Lichenstein in celluloid).

The interconnectedness of life and art for André Gide was deep and complex, as it was for Jasper Johns. Throughout his career, Johns quoted the art of the past, as well as his own. Like Edgar Degas (who, like Johns, was a brilliant draughtsman and also a sculptor in bronze), Johns related to the Old Masters and historical tradition (such as Matthias Grünewald). Just as Kasimir Malevich made references to the Byzantine ikon tradition and Brice Marden acknowledged Old Masters such as the Spanish painters Francisco de Zurbarán, Diego Velásquez, and Édouard Manet and Paul Cézanne, so Johns consciously quoted past artists.

Michael Fried, in a "New York Letter" of 1964, wrote that Frank Stella and Barnett Newman were 'historically self-aware' (1964, 59). Stella's acute (art) historical self-awareness came out very clearly in his book *Working Space*. Jasper Johns was less preachy, perhaps, but his historical self-awareness was very much to the fore.

By the time of *The Seasons* (mid-1980s), the examination of the private and public past reached its apotheosis in a series of autobiographical paintings. As Gide's novelist Edouard says: 'the history of the book will have interested me more than the book itself'.[17] Gide began his writing career by referring to the act of writing, just as Jasper Johns has always quoted *himself and* other artists. For instance, in his first work, *Paludes*, Gide's narrator included a space for the reader to add to a list of 'Most Remarkable Phrases'.[18] Later, Lawrence Durrell had the character

17 André Gide: *The Counterfeiters*, tr Dorothy Bussy, Penguin , 1966, 170

18 André Gide: *Paludes*, Secker & Warburg 1953, 95

Pursewarden place an asterisk in a novel which refers the reader to a blank page, and Durrell himself does this in his *The Alexandria Quartet.*

Jasper Johns too includes marks and references which the viewer can take up and run with, or not, as they wish. The references to the artist's own works re-inforces the fantasy world of the art itself, the secondary world which the art creates. Johns is also fashioning a history of his own art, as well as a commentary upon it. And this is certainly another reason why Johns' art is so popular with art critics,[19] because, like T.S. Eliot's *The Wasteland*, it is continuously commenting upon itself. The self-awareness is supremely modernist.

Contemporary with Jasper Johns's art in the 1960s was Samuel Beckett's exploration of self-referential art (Frank Stella and Richard Long are among many modern artists who have referred to Beckett's texts). Like Johns, Beckett plundered his back catalogue. Starting from the statement that there is 'nothing to express' and 'nothing with which to express', Beckett wrote a series of short, condensed pieces which he called 'fizzles', which have similarities with Johns' mirror games (Johns provided artworks to accompany Beckett's *Fizzles*).[20] Beckett's short fictions of the Sixties – *Ping, Lessness, Texts For Nothing, All Strange Away* and *Still* – with their mathematical descriptions of boxes, rotundas and cylinders, seem to be poetic equivalents of the smooth, rigid volumes of Minimal art in the 1960s (Donald Judd, Robert Morris, Carl Andre, Dan Flavin, etc).

This is an extract from *Still* (1975), a superbly poetic text, and the most tranquil in all of Samuel Beckett's *œuvre*:

> Bright at last close of a dark day the sun shines out at last and goes down. Sitting quite still at valley window normally turn head now and see it the sun low in the southwest sinking. Even get up certain moods and go stand by

---

19 Johns on responses to art: 'Everyone is of course free to interpret the work in his own way. I think seeing a picture is one thing and interpreting it is another.' And on the critics: 'I never wish for critics.'

20 Louis-Ferdinand Céline was another European modernist writer that Johns referred to – in his 1978 painting *Céline* (Basel), which included crosshatch and flagstone motifs.

western window quite still watching it sink and then the afterglow. Always quite still some reason some time past this hour at open window facing south in small upright wicker chair with armrests. Eyes stare out unseeing till first movement some time past close though unseeing still while still light.[21]

And this is from a late Samuel Beckett work, 1983's *Worstward Ho*, with evocations of nothingness and void, and a steady descent into darkness – always with the fading light in Beckett's writing:

Worsening words whose unknown. Whence unknown. At all costs unknown. Now for to say as worst they may only they only they. Dim void shades all they. Nothing save what they say. Somehow say. Nothing save they. What they say. Whosoever whence-soever say. As worst they may fail worse to say.
•
So leastward on. So long as dim still. Dim undimmed. Or dimmed to dimmer still. To dimmost dim. Leastmost in dimmost dim. Utmost dim. Leastmost in utmost dim. Unworsenable dim. (1992, 29, 33)

Like Jasper Johns, Samuel Beckett often employs the Minimalists' use of seriality, of doing one thing then another, in sequence. Artists such as Brice Marden, Sol LeWitt, Donald Judd and Carl Andre based some of their artworks on series of numbers or patterns. Minimal ethics can produce some extremes of mathematics and seriality. Andre's *37 Pieces of Work* is a good example of Minimal aesthetic permutations taken to extremes:

Taken as a whole *37 Pieces of Work* consists of 1,296 plates [wrote David Bourdon], 216 each of aluminium, copper, steel, magnesium, lead and zinc. Each metal appears alone in individual six-foot square plains. Then alternates with another, checkerboard fashion, in every possible permutation. Since each of the six metals in the large piece was laid out in the alphabetical order of its chemical symbol, alternating successively with the others, there are two versions of each combination[22]

Like Samuel Beckett and the Minimal artists, Jasper Johns moved calmly and methodically from one thing to another. Sol LeWitt (perhaps the

---

21 *Collected Shorter Prose 1945-1980*, Calder, 1984,183.

22 David Bourdon: *Carl Andre: Sculpture 1959-1977*, Jaap Rietman, New York, NY, 1978, 56. See Mel Bochner: "Serial Art Systems: Solipsism", *Arts Magazine*, vol. 41, no. 8, Summer 1967, 39-43

most extreme of the Minimalists, for all his work is done in the planning stage), believed that Johns used numbers, but not necessarily mathematics: not just

> anyone uses mathematics *per se*. They use *numbers*. It's just like Jasper Johns using, 1, 2, 3, 4, 5, 6, 7, 8, 9, 0. I use numbers only as a way of drawing something.[23]

Another European *avant garde* writer that Jasper Johns was influenced by was Ludwig Wittgenstein, the German philosopher best known for his work in the area of language and knowledge (for instance, in his *Tractus Logico-Philosophicus*, one of his key works, which has an influence outside of the world of philosophy). Ludwig Wittgenstein, Karl Kraus and Samuel Beckett wrote lucidly of the limits of language. Kraus, for example, echoed Stendhal, Gustave Flaubert and André Gide, in evoking a form of writing and literature which would be highly compressed and reductive – that is, reducing language to its essence, echoing the distillations of abstract art. For Wittgenstein, the limits of language are the limits of his world. In his *Tractatus Logico-Philosophicus*, Wittgenstein wrote:

> The world is *my* world; this is manifest in the fact that the limits of *language*... mean the limits of *my* world.[24]

---

23 Quoted in F. Colpitt, 63.

24 L. Wittgenstein: *Tractatus Logico-Philosophicus*, tr. D.F. Pears & B.F. McGuinness, Routledge & Kegan Paul 1961

3 : DO SOMETHING TO THE AMERICAN FLAG

I think that one wants from a painting a sense of life. The final suggestion, the final statement, has to be not a deliberate statement but a helpless statement. It has to be what you can't avoid saying.

Jasper Johns (1974, 14)

Jasper Johns was concerned with doing something different from other artists. He is a 'radical conservative', quite self-consciously reactionary. As he says:

> I had a feeling that I could do anything... But if I could do anything I wanted to do, then what I wanted to do was find out what I did that other people didn't, what I was that other people weren't... It was not a matter of joining a group effort, but of isolating myself from any group.[25]

Can an artist work wholly isolated and alone? No. But they can try.

The Johnsian motifs – the targets, flags, numbers and maps – are merely patterns or shapes which free the artist to explore other things. He is not interested in maps or flags or ale cans or numbers, but in plasticity,

---

25 J. Johns, quoted in D. Wheeler, 143

surface, colour, texture, form and other painterly concerns.

One of Jasper Johns' maxims was this:

Take an object
Do something to it
Do something else to it
" " " " (1965, 192)[26]

The motifs take care of certain elements in a work, so that the artist is free to look at other aspects. The aim is to create 'things which are seen and not looked at', Jasper Johns said, and explained further:

Using the design of the American flag took care of a great deal for me because I didn't have to design it. So I went on to similar things like the targets – things the mind already knows. That gave me room to work on other levels.[27]

The flags and targets are disarmingly simple forms, a formal reductionism that allows æsthetic expansion in other areas. As Max Kozloff wrote, the flags and targets were

merely so many abstract forms upon which social usage has conferred meaning, but which now, displaced into their new context, cease to function socially. From this tremendous insight alone have sprung the momentum of Pop Art and the huge quantities of abstraction that is emblematic in character (1962)

Jasper Johns' famous American *Flag* (1955, in the Museum of Modern Art in Gotham) is his signature artwork. *Flag* is a complex piece that opened up the way into Pop Art. *Flag* can be read in a number of ways, which seemingly conflict with each other. Johns explored the notions and relations between presentation and representation, between image and actuality, between iconography and abstraction.

---

26 An alternative quote is: 'Do something, do something to that, and then do something to that'.

27 In L. Steinberg, 1972, 31.

Jasper Johns' *Flag* is at once a banal icon (though for the America of the 1950s, as now, feelings of US nationalism, embodied in the American Stars and Stripes, were running high), and a complex piece of formal abstraction. With Johns' *Flag*, everyday signs and images, taken for granted, are treated with a grandeur of style and technique formerly employed by the great painters, the Old Masters.

Jasper Johns used the gestures of Abstract Expressionism, which aspire for grandeur and monumentality in painting, and gave them an ironic, self-reflexive twist. Johns produced a new sense of space which the art object inhabits. Rosalind Krauss writes:

> Johns' *Targets* or *Ale Cans*, in negating the internality of the abstract-expressionist picture, simultaneously rejects the innerness of its space and the privacy of the self for which that space was a model. His was a rejection of an ideal space that exists prior to experience, waiting to be filled, and of a psychological model in which a self exists replete with its meanings prior to contact with its world. (259)

The key to Jasper Johns' reworking of formalism and abstraction in the flags, targets, numbers and alphabets was precisely the sensuality of his art. It was the way he so powerfully employed the techniques of the Old Masters, of 'great art', that made his flags and targets so successful. Critics could not see Johns' banal signs culled from popular culture as trivial art, for Johns used one of the key elements in 'high art', the sensual, heavily impastoed surface. Johns' art could not be dismissed by critics, then as now, because its surface is as sensual and painterly as the art of Rembrandt van Rijn, Diego Velásquez or Titian.

In *Working Space*, his excellent series of art history lectures, Frank Stella discusses Michelangelo Merisi da Caravaggio's art, but he could just as well be speaking of Jasper Johns:

> The second miracle of Caravaggio is the miracle of surface. Skin, flesh, and pigment blend into reality. Painting is acknowledged as an act and as a physical fact, but immediately afterward, almost simultaneously, the presence of the human figure is felt as real, touchably there. (1)

William Rubin discusses the relation between Jasper Johns and Frank Stella, and the influence he had on Stella:

> there's a vast difference in sensibilities and in aims, so I don't want to make this relationship too close, but I think Johns also had one other importance. That is, his flag pictures and some of the other images he made were the first paintings in which the field of the pictures is absolutely identical with the motif of the picture: the boundaries of the pictures are identical with the boundaries of the flag. The flag is laid out as a flat pattern on the surface, and although Johns is a representational painter in that sense and Frank became an abstract painter, I think the notion of making the motif identical with the shape of the field, even though that shape remains rectangular in Johns' flag, lurks somewhere behind what would become the principle of Frank's shaped canvas. And that principle is, if I can define it in its simplest way, essentially that the boundary of the picture is going to be determined by the governing pattern of the surface, and that there will be an absolute reciprocity between the outer shape of the picture, which might be considered simply the outside line of a pattern that operates over the entire surface.[28]

---

28 In E. De Antonio, 138-9.

4 : REAL THINGS

I don't know how to organise thoughts. I don't know how to have thoughts.

Jasper Johns

Paintings by Jasper Johns such as 1955's *White Flag* ('the most blatantly sensuous canvas Johns has ever produced', commented his friend Michael Crichton [1977, 131]), or *Good Time Charley* (1961),29 are full of an erotic pleasure in surface, a feeling for touch that pretty much surpasses that of just about any other contemporary artist. The later works by Johns are full of sensual pleasures.30 Pieces such as *Book* (1957), a real book covered in a thick layer of wax and oil, are positively voluptuous in their haptic sensibility.31 When Johns folds or mixes in bits of newspaper or stencils or different objects – such as rulers, wires, frames, cups or casts – the result is even more extraordinary. Works such as *Untitled* mesh a number of panels

29 *Good Time Charley*, 1961, encaustic on canvas with objects, 38 x 24in, collection: the artist

30 J. Johns: *Dancers on a Plane*, 1979, oil on canvas with objects, 78 x 64in, private collection, New York, NY

31 *Book*, 1957, encaustic with objects, 25.4 x 33cm, private collection, New York, NY

with sticks of wood and other objects which are stuck directly on top of the canvas.32 As with Robert Rauschenberg's art (by way of the Cubists), these stuck-on objects set alight the painting.

Jasper Johns explains why he uses 'real objects' glued onto his paintings:

> My thinking is perhaps dependent on a realization of a thing as being the real thing... I like what I see to be real, or to be my idea of what is real. And I think I have a kind of resentment against illusion when I can recognize it. Also, a large part of my work has been involved with the painting as object, as real thing in itself. And in the face of that 'tragedy,' so far, my general development... has moved in the direction of using real things as painting. That is to say I find it more interesting to use a real fork as painting than it is to use painting as a real fork.33

Much of Jasper Johns' art explored æsthetic issues in a seemingly child-like manner. As Johns spoke about using oil and wax because it dries quickly, so he explored colour and the relation of colours to their names. He was interested in the *idea* of colour, of colour as a means of communication, and how it is conditioned by cultural factors.34

In *False Start* (1959), Jasper Johns painted splodges of yellow and stencilled the word WHITE over them.35 He stencilled ORANGE in white letters over a patch of bright red. His aim, he said, was to find other ways of using colour:

> The flags and targets have colors positioned in a predetermined way. I wanted to find a way to apply color so that the color would be determined by some

---

32 *Untitled*, 1972, oil, encaustic and collage on canvas with objects, 183 x 487.7cm, Museum Ludwig, Cologne

33 Quoted in D. Sylvester, op. cit., 15-16.

34 'I have no ideas about what the paintings imply about the world. I don't think that's a painter's business. He just paints paintings without a conscious reason.'

35 J. Johns: *False Start*, 1959, oil on canvas, 5.6 x 4.4ft, collection: S.I. Newhouse, Jr., New York, NY

other method.[36]

The result is a painting that aims to go beyond visual pleasure, to become an ironic comment on perception and conceptualization. Jasper Johns creates, as critic Barbara Rose noted in a 1976 article, "Decoys and Doubles: Jasper Johns and the Modernist Mind", a metaphysics of art, which does not separate art from life, or æsthetics from experience.[37] Again, this is a common philosophical view in modern art – that art and life combine.[38] Or that art is inseparable from life. It's André Gide's idea again, living life and as he's living it, being aware of how he can transmute his experiences into art.

36 Quoted in D. Wheeler, 136.

37 See Barbara Rose, 1976, 68-73; 1977, 148-153.

38 'When something is new to us,' Jasper Johns noted, 'we treat it as an experience. We feel that our senses are awake and clear. We are alive. As one gets older one sees many more paths that could be taken. Artists sense within their own work that kind of swelling of possibilities, which may seem a freedom or a confusion.'

5 : *THE SEASONS*

Sometimes I see it and then paint it. Other times I paint it and then see it.
Both are impure situations, and I prefer neither.

Jasper Johns

The late works of Jasper Johns excite critics such as Robert Rosenblum,
who adores Johns' series of mid-Eighties paintings, *The Seasons* (1985-
86).[39] Rosenblum writes of Johns' paintings:

> The Johns' paintings, the quartet of the cycle of the four seasons are just
> heart-breakingly intimate tragic comments on the passing of time, nature,
> personal biography and so on. As such they really seem to extend the great
> tradition of the history of Western art, in particular of romantic identity with
> nature... [the paintings] seem to be personal projections of his own life viewed
> against the passing seasons. That's a traditional theme, God knows, in Western
> art. The pictures not only have that universal aspect of going from spring to
> winter but also all kinds of cryptic as well as decipherable references to his
> own art, biography, and past. They're very meditative, they're like the works of
> some late great poet who is contemplating his life, his career, his future
> against the aspect of eternity. They really are very directly moving in the
> grand old tradition...

39 J. Johns: *Spring, Summer, Autumn, Winter*, 1985-86, each encaustic on canvas,
75 x 50in, collection: S.I. Newhouse, New York, NY; collection: Philip Johnson;
collection: the artist; collection: Asher B. Edelman and Mildred Ash. See J. Russell,
1987; B. Rose, 1987, 192f; J. Goldman, 1987

There are works where Jasper Johns consciously addresses erotic issues, such as in the *Skin* drawings (1973), mentioned above, where he takes an image of his own genitals (other artists who have drawn their penis include Egon Schiele and Eric Gill). In his famous *Target with Plaster Casts* of 1955,[40] Johns placed under the little trapdoors parts of the human (male) body including, of course, the penis. The *Painting with Two Balls* of 1960 is just that: a canvas split across its width with two balls stuck in the crack.[41] In a later piece, the *Tantric Detail* drawing of 1980, Johns placed a pair of testicles in the same place as the two balls in the 1960 *Painting*.

There is an undercurrent of homoeroticism in Jasper Johns' art which critics have only rarely addressed fully.[42] And there is a biographical aspect to this: for example, Johns' relationship with the artist Robert Rauschenberg.

---

40 J. Johns: *Target with Plaster Casts,* 1955, encaustic & collage on canvas with objects, collection: Leo Castelli, New York, NY

41 J. Johns: *Painting with Two Balls,* 1960, encaustic and collage on canvas with objects, 65 x 54in, collection: the artist

42 See J. Cuno, 1987, 92; R. Feinstein, 1980, 139-143; M. Rosenthal, 48f.

6 : CROSSHATCH

I often find that having an idea in my head prevents me from doing something else. Working is therefore a way of getting rid of an idea.

Jasper Johns

Later works by Jasper Johns did things such as playfully stick genitals onto paintings, such as the 1980 *Dancers on a Plane*.[43] Johns said he was influenced by 'Tantric paintings in which Shiva and Shakti copulate, representing the inter-penetration of destructive and creative forces.'[44] So Johns turns East, like millions of other Western artists. One might see Johns' 'crosshatch' paintings, with their energetic, mobile and very painterly marks, as a form of a cosmic, religious dance. Dancing itself is course profoundly erotic. As the Frank Sinatra puts it, 'what is dancing but making love set to music?'

Jasper Johns' art can be as stunning and sensuous in his pencil

---

43 J. Johns: *Dancers on a Plane*, 1980, oil on canvas with painted bronze frame and objects, 200 x 162cm, Tate Modern, London

44 J. Johns in 1987, quoted in Mark Rosenthal, 44

drawings and lithographs.[45] Few contemporary works of art are as thrilling as those densely-shaded sketches, where the crosshatching is thick and makes deep black squares and rectangles, as in *Coat Hanger* (1960), *Flag* (1957), and *Device Circle* (1960).[46] These deeply dark squares and shapes are exquisite – their total presence is simultaneously religious and erotic. They recall the magic squares of Robert Fludd, a Renaissance alchemist (1574-1637), such as the small black square, a mass of lines and crosshatching, which has *Et sic infinitum* written along each of the four sides. Fludd's magic square is an alchemical statement on the original chaos before life began, but it is also a beautiful object, that drawing, whose impact stems from a tactile presence and sense of pleasure.[47] It is the same with other alchemical texts which depict primal chaos, as in the entropy image of Coenders van Helpen.[48]

These alchemical visions of primal matter, the *nigredo* or blackness of the *opus alchymicum*, are clearly related to womb imagery, to the great cosmic darkness of the Goddess as Great Mother, the *regressus ad uterum* which is a primal desire in Jungian psychology, to get back to the womb.[49] These black magic squares are seen now by critics as forerunners of modern abstraction – as precursors of Kasimir Malevich's red and black squares, or the five-foot black squares of Ad Reinhardt and other Abstract

---

45 See R. Castleman, 1986; M. Field, 1970; C. Geelhaar, 1980; D. Shapiro, 1984, J. Goldman.

46 *Coat Hanger I*, 1960, lithograph, 91.4 x 67.9cm, edition of 35, Universal Limited Art Editions; *Flag*, 1957, pencil on paper, 27.6 x 38.9cm, collection: the artist; *Device Circle*, 1960, pencil on paper, 38 x 37cm, collection: Ronald S. Lauder.

47 Robert Fludd: *Utriusque cosmi maioris scilicet et minoris metaphysica, physica atque technica historia*, Oppenheim 1617, I, 26

48 Coenders van Helpen, Barent: *Tresor de la philosophie des ancients*, cologne 1693, 29

49 see Johannes Fabricus: *Alchemy: The Medieval Alchemists and Their Royal Art*, Aquarian Press, 1989, 98f

Expressionists.50

The whole of Jasper Johns' work can be viewed as sculpture, as an exploration of the relation between 'real' objects and their representation ('I tend to like things that already exist'), an exploration of the links between imagination, fantasy, memory, image, representation and perception. The late works by Johns quote from earlier works, in complex ways. In a number of late works, Johns places a plaster cast of an arm, his arm, the artist's arm, reaching for the artist's tools, perhaps.51 The arm – the hand especially – connotes the creative ability of the artist, the human touch, the creative Hand of God, in effect, which, as it reaches down from the top of Johns' mixed media paintings, is clearly a controlling force. Yet, at the same time, the arm is dismembered, fragmented, a sign pointing towards a world of creativity and humanity that is elsewhere.

The late works by Jasper Johns that quote earlier works explore the relation between personal history and art history, between notions of an artistic career and its representation, between the poetics of memory and the memory of poetics, art as mnemonic poetry.52

Jasper Johns' bronze sculptures, echoing the work of Marcel Duchamp, Kurt Schwitters and Max Ernst, represent 'real' objects – ale cans, lightbulbs, shoes.53 Whatever the æsthetics of the sculptures – with

50 see Hugh Cumming: "Abstract Painting and the Spiritual" and "The Spiritual in Art: Abstract Painting: Charles Jencks interviews Maurice Tuchman", in A.C. Papadakis, 1987, 19f, 42

51 J. Johns: *In the Studio*, 1982, encaustic and collage on canvas with objects, 72 x 48in, collection: the artist; *Perilous Night*, 1982, encaustic on canvas with objects, collection: Robert & Jane Meyerhoff, Phoenix, Maryland; *Untitled*, 1983, encaustic and collage on canvas with objects, 48.2 x 75.2in, collection: S.I. Newhouse, Jr., New York, NY

52 J. Johns: *Racing Thoughts*, 1983, encaustic & collage on canvas, 48 x 75.2in, Whitney Museum of American Art, New York; *Ventriloquist*, 1983, encaustic on canvas, 75 x 50in, Museum of Fine Arts, Houston, TX

53 J. Johns: *Ale Cans*, 1964, painted bronze, 3 x 6 x 2in, Leo Castelli Gallery, New York, NY; *English Lightbulb*, 1968-70, metal, wire, polyvinylchloride, 5 x 3in, Leo Castelli Gallery, New York, NY; *High School Days*, 1964, 12in, collection: the artist

their complex explorations of the relations between reality, image, form and space – they are sumptuous objects.

Jasper Johns' bronze sculptures are even more exciting, in terms of texture and touch, than his paintings: his bronze *Flag* (1960) is crushingly beautiful, as wonderful a work of art as was ever produced by anybody anywhere.[54]

It's just bronze. It's just an image of a flag. But it does so much more.

---

54 *Flag*, 1960, bronze, 31.1 x 47.6cm, collection: the artist

7 : JASPER JOHNS
AND CONTEMPORARY ARTISTS

There are many other contemporary artists who have developed an acute sense of surface and texture, some of these surfaces deriving in part from Jasper Johns, and some not: among the more successful are painters such as Christopher Le Brun, Anselm Keifer (such as in his *Wayland's Song*[55]), Thérèse Oulton, Lance Smith, Hughie O'Donoghue, R. B. Kitaj, Jim Dine and Richard Diebenkorn. Painters who seem to have a direct Johnsian component in their art include Frank Stella, Brice Marden, Sean Scully, Howard Hodgkin and Gerard Richter. The Minimal sculptors – Donald Judd, Robert Morris and Carl Andre – have acknowledged Johns', as well as Frank Stella's importance.[56]

Among contemporary artists, however, Jasper Johns seems to be the king of surface. He can handle any medium. It seems he can apply anything to his works and remain dazzling. Very few artists are as sexy in

55 Anselm Keifer: *Wayland's Song (With Wing)*, 1982, oil, emulsion, straw on photo, on canvas with lead

56 On Jasper Johns and Robert Morris, see Barbara Rose: "New York Letter", *Art International*, vol. 7, no. 9, Dec 1963, 63; Sidney Tillim: "New York Exhibitions", *Arts Magazine*, vol. 38, no. 3, Dec 1963, 62; Lucy Lippard: "New York Letter", *Art International*, vol. 9, no. 4, May 1965, 57

their use of materials. One thinks of Frank Stella, who was certainly influenced by Johns, as William Rubin notes:

> Frank was, I think, very interested in Johns' work in his last months at Princeton and immediately after he graduated. Johns' flags would be the pictures we'd have to look to in that sense, because they provided a concept of a picture that would be striped, as these pictures are, and also where the stars are a kind of box, which is not unrelated to the box in the center of *Coney Island*. Johns' pictures interested Frank because of certain repetition, repetition of numbers or letters or stripes of the flag, and Frank saw possibilities in this repetition which Johns himself was not to see.[57]

Since the 1970s and his *Indian Birds* series, Frank Stella has been building his paintings out from the wall, so that they become deliriously three-dimensional, though Stella claims they remain 'paintings', not sculptures. Stella's new works are as exuberant and as colourful as art can be. They are so startlingly in their sheer pleasure and enthusiasm that some people could be put off by them, observing them with suspicion. Works such as *Thruxton 3X* (1982) are explosions of light, colour, texture, shape, pattern, volume, space and multi-media extravagance.[58] Works such as *Diavolozoppo* (1984) are constructed out of as many materials as the painter can get his hands on.[59] *The Try Works* (1988) employs huge slabs of aluminium pressed into elaborate French curves, layered over each other, painted in wild red, blues and pinks.[60]

There is no illusion in Frank Stella's works, as in many of Jasper Johns' works: they are not depicting anything other than themselves, with their squiggles and zigzags patterns, their fluorescent pinks and lurid greens,

---

57 Quoted in E. De Antonio, 138.

58 Frank Stella: *Thruxton 3X,* 1982, mixed media on etched aluminium, 75 x 85 x 15 in, Shidler Collection, Honolulu

59 Frank Stella: *Diavolozoppo,* 1984, oil, urethane enamel, fluorescent alkyd, acrylic, and printing ink on canvas, etched magnesium, aluminium and fibreglass, 139 x 170 x 16in, collection: the artist

60 Frank Stella: *The Try Works (B-6, 2X)*, 1988, mixed media on cast aluminium, 281.3 x 235 private collection

their splotches and dabs and overpainting. Stella says:

> My painting is based on the fact that only what can be seen there *is* there. It really is an object... All I want anyone to get out of my paintings, and all I ever get out of them, is the fact that you see the whole idea without any confusion... What you see is what you see.[61]

Many contemporary painters are self-consciously loose and messy – think of John Walker, Michael Porter, Amat, K.H. Hodicke, Enzo Cucchi and Francis Bacon. Freudians have things to say about artists who are deliberately 'messy' – for them it all goes back to anal psychology, toilet training and constipation. Aesthetically, the explosion into chaos and mess helps to renew the connection, as Frank Stella says, with the eroticism of texture, with the sexuality of surface, which has always been a large part of art. Think of Greek sculpture: the smoothness of the marble and stone is crucial to the overall experience of the statue. Similarly with Italian Renaissance painting, with all the punched and embossed gold, which provides the spaceless, divine background to Jesus and the Virgin in so many altarpieces and panels.

Other artists who have explored the sensuality of surfaces include Robert Ryman, with his sumptuous white-on-white squares. Ad Reinhardt painted black-on-black squares (though Robert Rauschenberg had painted all-black paintings before Reinhardt). Jasper Johns' use of gray, and Reinhardt's and Rauschenberg's of black, influenced other monochrome painters, such as Brice Marden, Frank Stella, Jules Olitski and Ryman.[62]

Robert Ryman explored the mysticality of white-on-white, as Kasimir

---

61 Frank Stella, radio broadcast, 1964, in G. Battock, 158. See Robert Rosenblum: *Frank Stella*, Penguin 1971; William S. Rubin: *Frank Stella*, New York Graphic Society, Greenwich, CT, 1970; "Frank Stella: Portrait of the Artist as an Image Administrator", *Art in America*, Feb 1985, 94-107; and "Frank Stella and the Simulacrum", *Flash Art*, Feb-March 1986, 32-5

62 See Brenda Richardson: *Frank Stella: The Black Paintings*, Baltimore Museum of Art, Baltimore 1976, 3; F. Colpitt, 29

Malevich had done.63 Paintings of Ryman's such *Untitled*, a small painting by contemporary standards (53.5 inches square), or the very small *Untitled* of 1961 (12 inches square), display a sense of the tactile to rival Jasper Johns.

Robert Ryman's art, like Jasper Johns', is founded on the sensuality of paint, of surfaces, of the eroticism of texture. By limiting himself to white, Ryman frees himself up for an exploration of different media, for he paints in white on many kinds of material: canvas, linen, cotton, wood, paper, steel, copper, aluminium, mylar, fibreglass, Plexiglass, cardboard, etc, and with different sorts of media: oil, baked enamel, paper, vinyl acetate emulsion, etc. As Ryman says, typically of so many contemporary artists: '[t]here is never a question of what to paint, but only how to paint'.64

Other post-painterly abstract artists who emphasize the sensuality of surface in their works include Brice Marden, with his post-Johnsian oil and wax panels; Jean Dubuffet and Antoni Tapiès love to crowd their surfaces with mixtures of materials;65 Anselm Keifer sticks bits of straw onto his oil paintings, using 'real things' as Johns advocated.66 Sean Scully's painterly surfaces recall Jasper Johns' oil and wax treatments, as do those of Howard Hodgkin; Scully's formal innovations with a small separate square canvas pushed into a larger set of panels bolted together also recalls Johns' multi-part paintings.

There many artists who use multiple panels or 3-D paintings that more

---

63 R. Ryman: *Department*, 1981, oil on aluminium, 60 x 60in, collection: Rhona J. Hoffman, Chicago. See Carlo Huber: *Robert Ryman*, Kunsthalle, Basel; Nancy Grimes: "Robert Ryman's White Magic", *Art News*, Summer 1968,86-92; Carter Ratcliff: "Robert Ryman Making Distinctions", *Art in America*, June 1986, 92-97

64 In D. Wheeler, 207.

65 Antoni Tapiès: *Great Painting*, 1958, oil and sand on canvas, 6"6' x 8'7', Guggenheim Museum, New York, NY; J. Dubuffet: *Run Grass, Jump Pebbles*, 1956, oil on canvas (assemblage), 6'8" x 5'1", private collection, Paris

66 Anselm Keifer: *Margarethe*, 1981, oil and straw on canvas, 9'2" x 12'6", Saatchi Collection, London; *Nurnberg-Festspiel-Weise*, 1981, oil, straw, mixed media on canvas, 9'2" x 12'6", collection; Eli & Edythe L. Broad, Los Angeles

than rival Jasper Johns' multi-part paintings: Elizabeth Murray, for instance, produces marvellous shaped panels.[67] Sam Gillam creates complexly shaped 'paintings' which gleefully smash the primacy of the traditional rectangle in painting;[68] Jennifer Bartlett has explored the dynamics of perception and space using multiple panels and rainbow-curved canvases;[69] Robert Mangold explores colour and architecture in his multi-panelled paintings which often contain a unifying element of drawing;[70] and Judy Pfaff's multi-media installations are riots of colour and materials which out-distance older artists such as Johns, Marden and Stella in scale and madness.[71]

Of course, one can extend sensuality in painting to any aspect of it: to colour for instance. Painters such as Helen Frankenthaler rejoice in the exuberance of pure colour.[72] Morris Louis poured paint directly onto the canvas to produce his deeply saturated furls, blotches and curtains of

67 Elizabeth Murray: *Simple Meaning*, 1982, oil on two canvases, 107 x 96in, collection: Jerry & Emily Spiegel, New York, NY; *Fire Cup*, 1982, oil on canvas, each canvas 92 x 82in, Paula Cooper Gallery, New York, NY. See Paul Gardner: "Elizabeth Murray Shapes Up", *Art News*, Sept 1984, 47-55; Roberta Smith: *Elizabeth Murray*, Dallas Museum of Art 1987

68 Sam Gillam: *Like Today*, 1985, acrylic on canvas with aluminium construction, 55 x 67 x 4in, Monique Knowlton Gallery, New York, NY

69 Jennifer Bartlett: *Horizon*, 1979, enamel, silkscreen and baked enamel on steel plates, oil on canvas, 20 plates, 1 canvas, 48 x 250in, collection: Martin Sklar, New York, NY. See J. Russell: *In the Garden*, Abrams, New York, NY, 1982; M. Goldwater *et al*: *Jennifer Bartlett*, Abbeville Press, New York, NY, 1985

70 Robert Mangold: *Four Color Frame Painting no. 1*, acrylic and pencil on canvas, 111 x 105in, collection: Martin Sklar, New York

71 Judy Pfaff: *N.Y.C.-B.Q.E, 1987*, painted steel, plastic laminates, fibreglass and wood, 15 x 35 x 5 feet, Max Protetch Gallery, New York, NY

72 Helen Frankenthaler: *Moveable Blue*, 1973, acrylic on canvas, 5'10" x 20'3", Citizens Fidelity Bank and Trust Company, Louisville; *Nature Abhors a Vacuum*, 1973, acrylic on canvas, 104 x 113in, Andre Emmerich Gallery, New York, NY

colour (in paintings such as *Aleph, Alpha-Delta* and *Saraband*).[73] Colour
has been central to contemporary artists such as Barnett Newman, Clyfford
Still, Christopher le Brun, Gillian Ayres, Howard Hodgkin, Kenneth Noland,
Jules Olitski and Joseph Albers.

What this shows, this emphasis on the sensuality of surface, colour
and other formal elements of painting, is that painting's eroticism is crucial
to its effect. This is very true of Jasper Johns' art. Without this eroticism of
colour, surface, texture, shape, pattern and form, painting loses much of its
impact. Art historians call this eroticism of form 'beauty', that old Platonic
word for all that is desirable. What 'beauty' means is precisely this
experience of the eroticism of the painting-as-object. The word 'beauty' too
is distinctly feminized in art criticism, for the 'beauty' of a painting is a
'feminine' quality; the painting is thus equivalent to a woman. The more a
painting reveals its sensuality, the more 'beautiful' it will be. With Jasper
Johns' art, this revelation of beauty is unleashed to the maximum, so that
people drool over Johns's paintings as they drool over the works of
Rembrandt van Rijn or Titian.

Jasper Johns continues to work – work is always the central fact of
artists' lives: 'I am just trying to find a way to make pictures', he has said.
One of Johns' best statements occurs in Emile De Antonio's documentary
film, and collected in the book *Painters Painting*:

> A lot of people have said that painting is dead, but people continue to work...
> (E. De Antonio, 163)

73 Morris Louis: *Alpha-Delta*, 1961, acrylic on canvas, 104 x 240in, Everson
Museum of Art, New York; *Saraband*, 1959, acrylic on canvas, 101 x 149in,
Guggenheim Museum, New York; *Aleph*, 1960, magna acrylic, 105 x 93in,
collection: del Amo, Madrid

ILLUSTRATIONS

On the following pages are some of the artists and works that have influenced Jasper Johns.

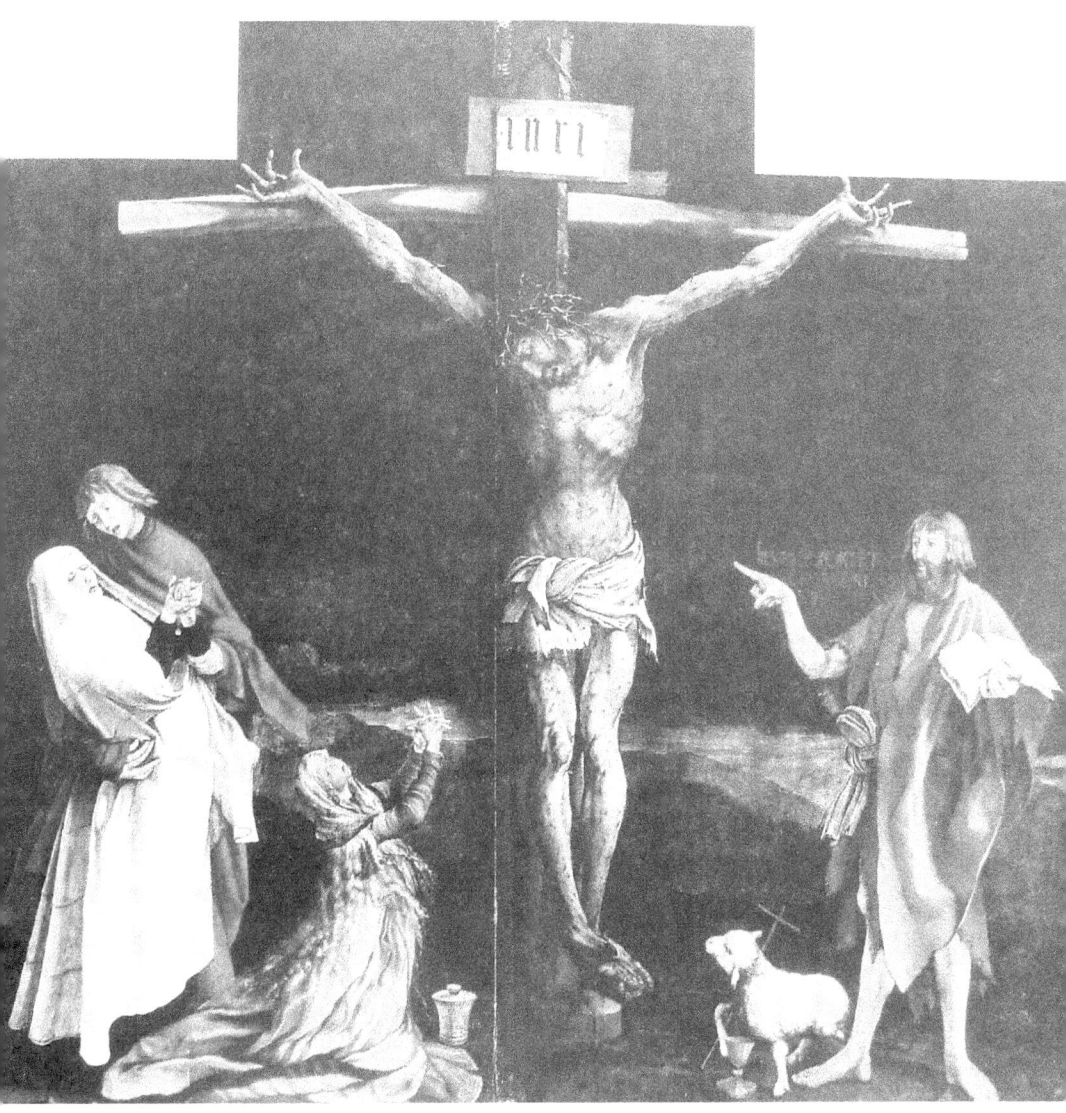

Matthias Grünewald, Crucifixion, Isenheim Altarpiece

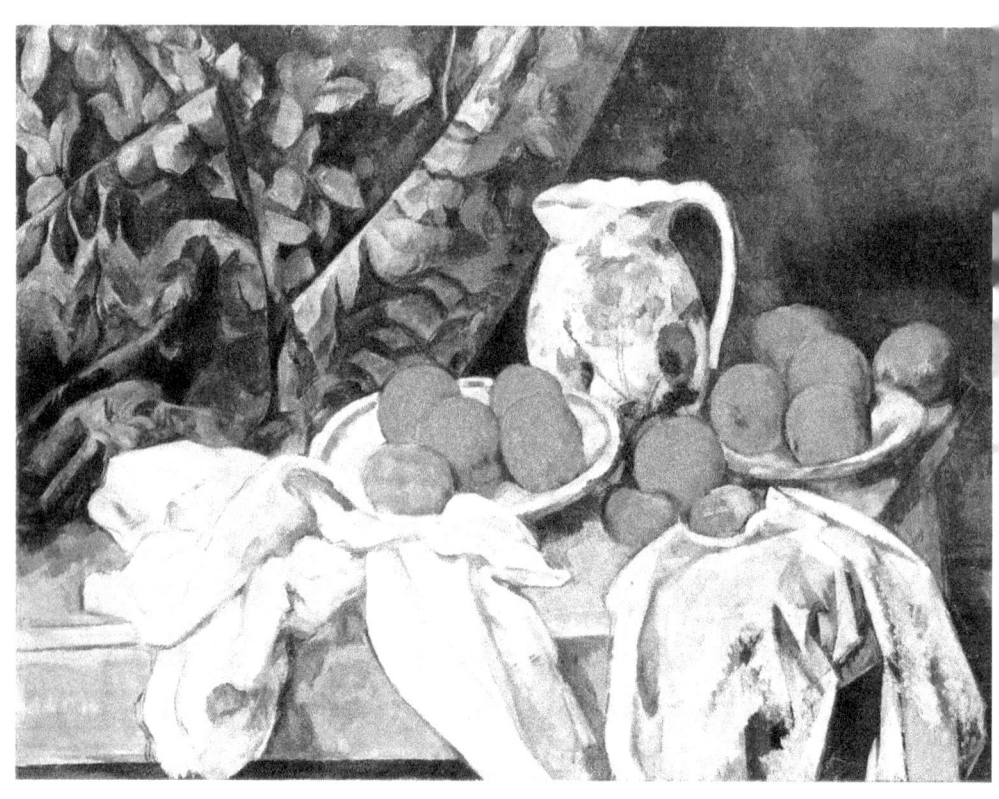

Paul Cézanne, Still Life with Curtain and Flowered Pitcher, c. 1899

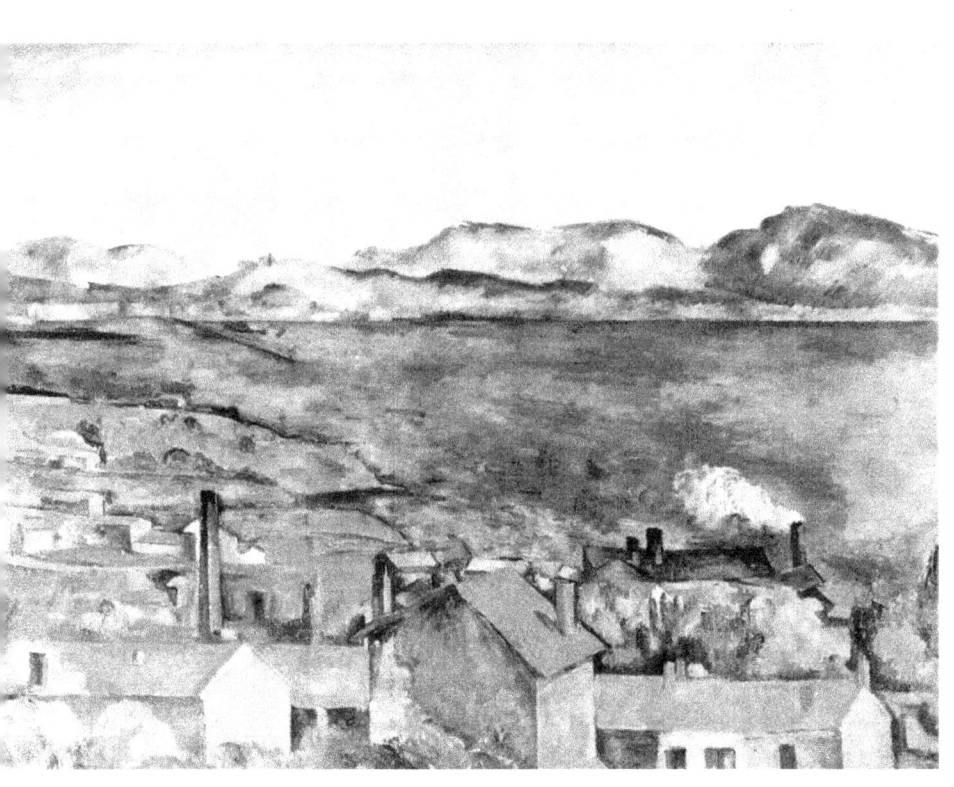

Paul Cézanne, The Bay From L'Estaque, c. 1886, Chicago

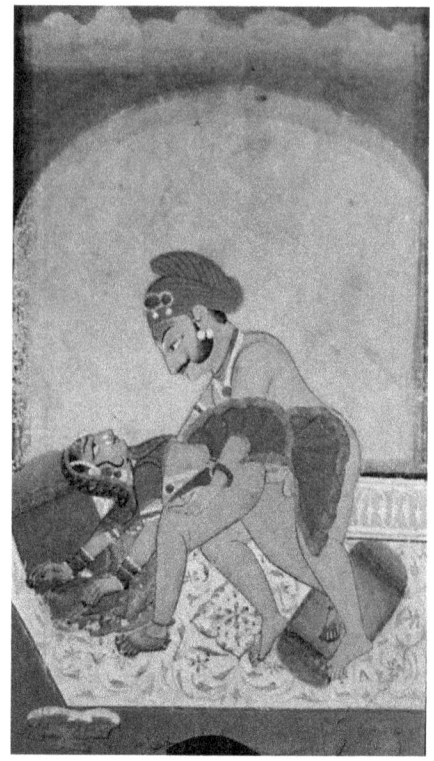

Indian erotic art:
Rajput, late 18th century, above.
Mogul style, 18th century, below.

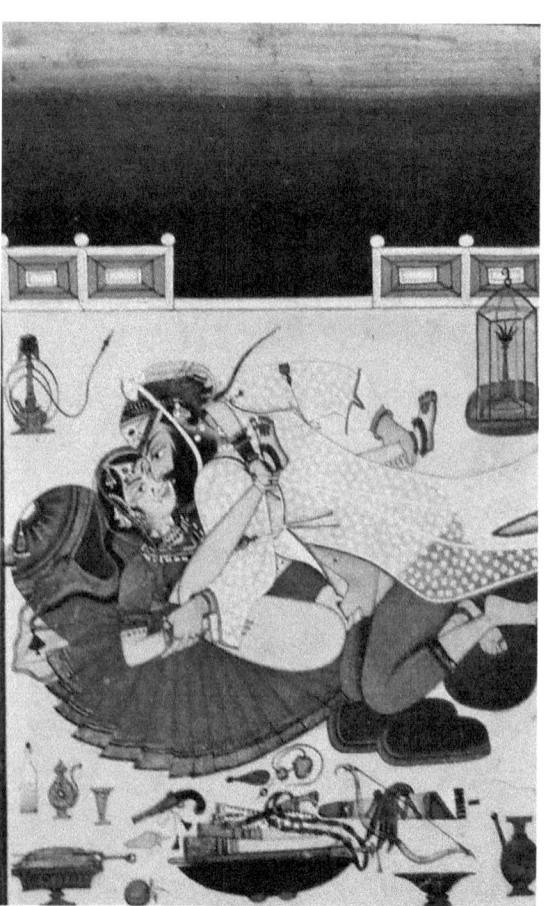

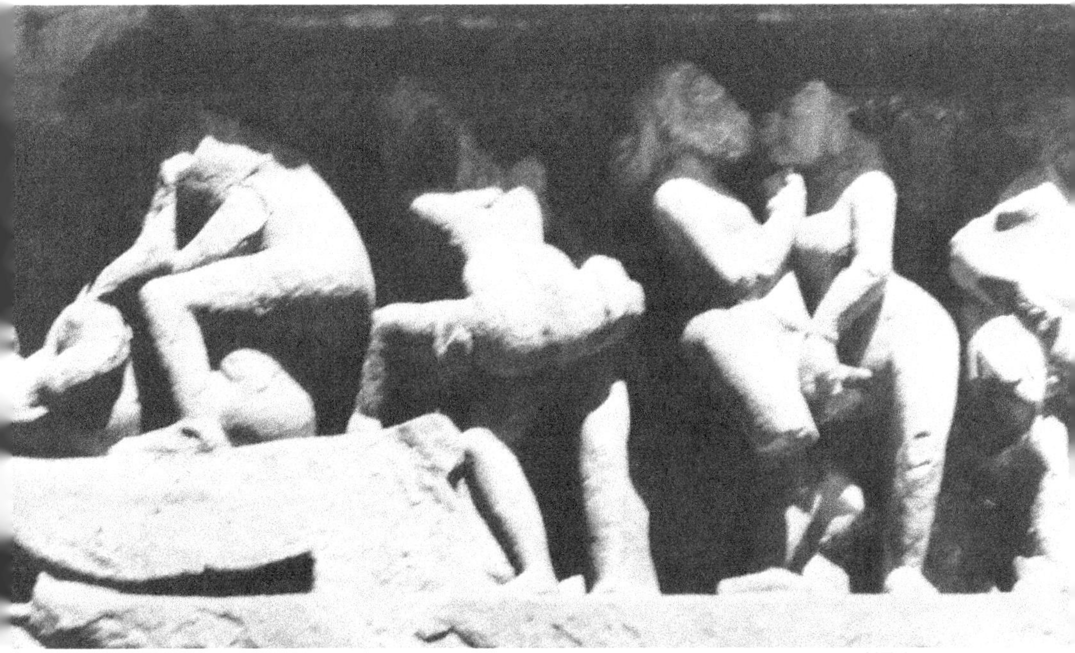

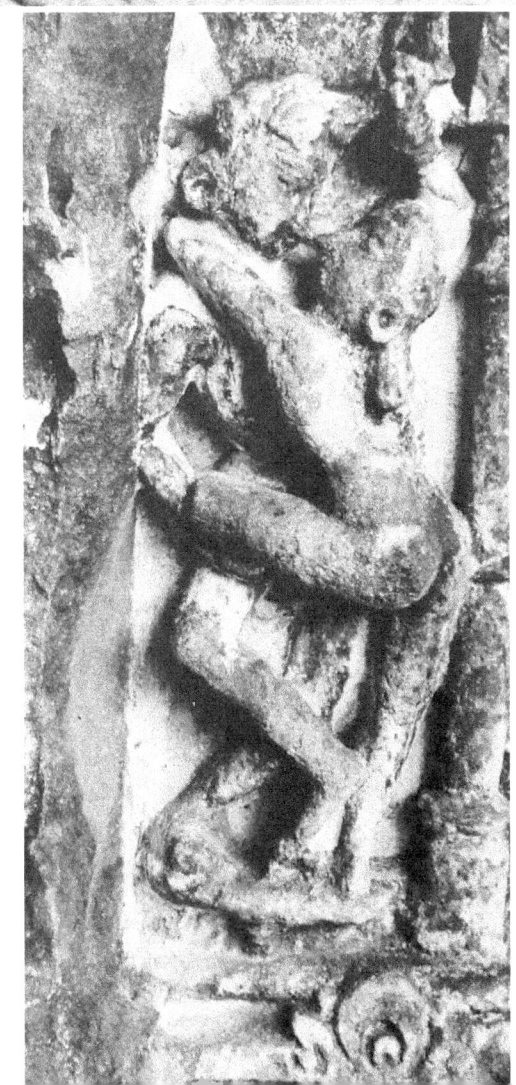

Khajuraho temple, 9-11 century,
Northern India, right.

Temple, 11th century, Mount Abu
area, Northern India

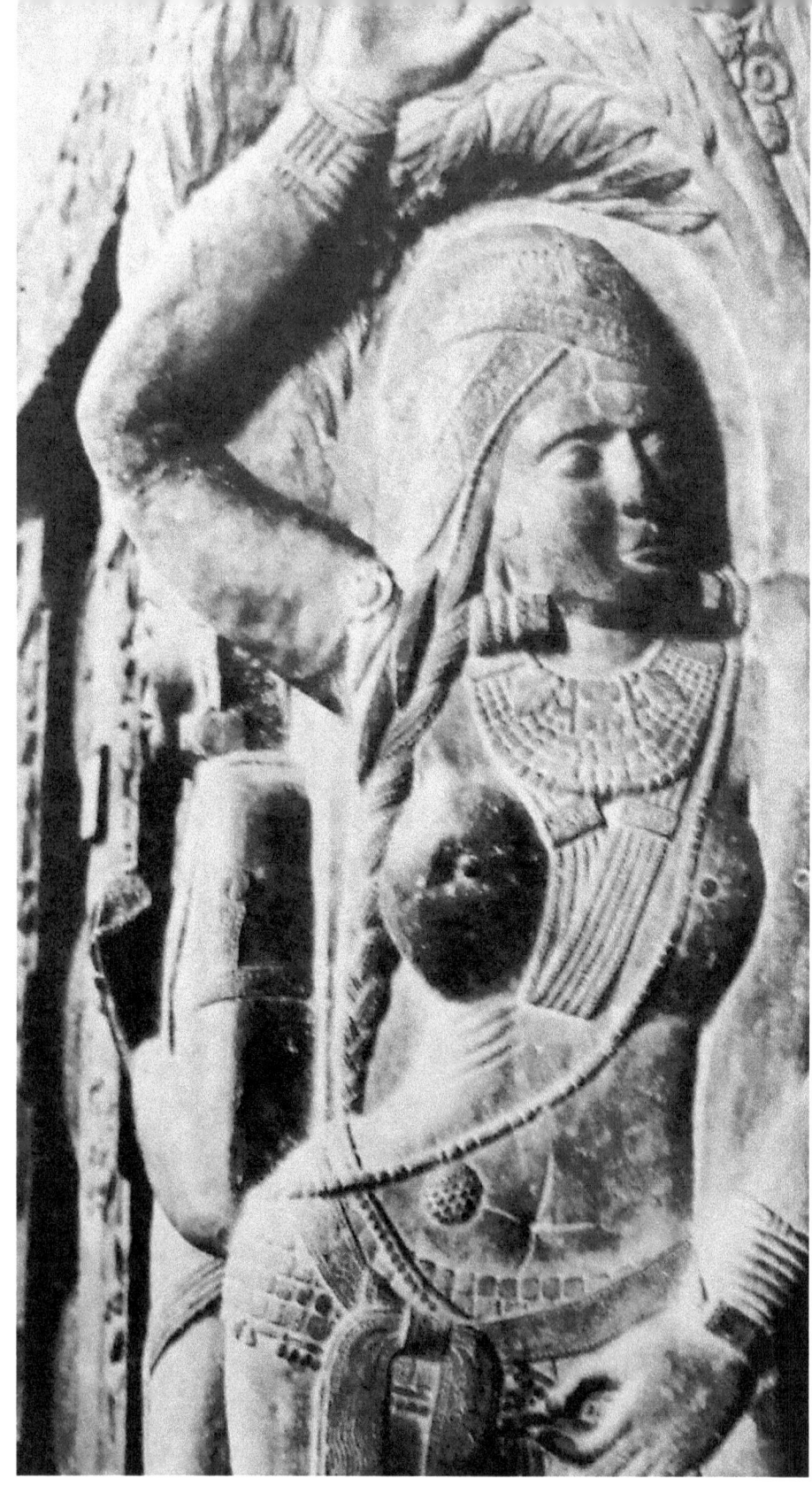

Yakshi figure, Indian Museum, Caluctta

BIBLIOGRAPHY

D. Anfam.
   Abstract Expressionism, Thames & Hudson, London, 1990
Emile de Antonio & Mitch Tuchman.
   Painters Painting, Abbeville Press, New York, NY, 1984
M. Archer.
   Art Since 1960, Thames & Hudson, London, 1997
Dore Ashton.
   American Art Since 1945, Thames & Hudson, London, 1982
Gregory Battock, ed.
   Minimal Art: A Critical anthology, Studio Vista, London, 1969
Germain Bazin.
   A Concise History of World Sculpture, David & Charles, Newton Abbot 1981
Samuel Beckett. *Collected Shorter Prose 1945-1980*, Calder 1984
   —. *Nohow On*, Calder 1992
Robert Bernstein.
   Jasper Johns' Paintings and Sculptures 1954-1974, Ann Arbor, MI, 1985
   —. & Lilian Tone, Jasper Johns, and Kirk Varnedoe. *Jasper Johns: A Retrospective*, Museum of Modern Art, New York, NY, 2006
Nicolas & Elena Calas.
   Icons and Image of the Sixties, Dutton, New York, NY, 1971
Riva Castleman.
   Jasper Johns: A Print Retrospective, Little, Brown, New York, NY, 1986
Herschel B. Chipp, ed.
   Theories of Modern Art, University Press of California, Los Angeles 1968
Frances Colpitt.
   Minimal Art: The Critical Perspective, University of Washington Press, Seattle, WA, 1990
Catherine Craft and Parkstone.
   Jasper Johns, Temporis Collection, 2009
M. Crichton.

Jasper Johns, Thames & Hudson, London, 1977
James Cuno.
    "Jasper Johns", *Print Quarterly*, vol. 4 no. 1, March 1987, 92
Jean-Luc Daval.
    History of Abstract Painting, Art Data, London, 1989
Roni Feinstein.
    "New Thoughts for Jasper Johns' Sculpture", *Arts Magazine*, vol. 54, no. 8, April 1980
Richard Field.
    Jasper Johns: Prints 1960-1970, Praeger 1970
Richard Francis.
    Jasper Johns, New York, NY, 1984/ 1990
M. Fried.
    "New York Letter", *Art International*, vol. 8, no. 3, April 1964
P. Fuller.
    "Jasper Johns Interviewed", *Art Monthly*, no. 18, July 1978
Christian Geelhaar.
    Jasper Johns: Working Proofs, Peterborough 1980
André Gide.
    The Counterfeiters, tr. Dorothy Bussy, Penguin, London, 1966
    —. *Logbook of The Coiners*, tr. Justin O'Brien, Cassell, London, 1952
Judith Goldman.
    Jasper Johns: Prints 1977-1981, Thomas Segal Gallery, Boston
    —. *Jasper Johns: The Seasons*, Leo Castelli Gallery, New York, NY, 1987
Robert Goldwater & Marco Treves, eds.
    Artists on Art, John Murray, London, 1975
Barbara Hess.
    Jasper Johns: The Business of the Eye, Taschen Basic Art Series, 2007)
Klaus Honnef.
    Contemporary Art, Benedikt Taschen, Cologne 1988
Sam Hunter, ed.
    An American Renaissance: Painting and Sculpture Since 1940, Abbeville Press, New York, NY, 1986
    —. *American Art of the 20th Century*, Thames & Hudson, London, 1973
Waldemar Januszczak, ed.
    Techniques of the World's Great Painters, Phaidon 1980
Jasper Johns.
    "Sketchbook Notes", in *Art and Literature*, 4, Lausanne, Spring 1965
    —. "Interview", *Jasper Johns Drawings*, Museum of Modern Art, Oxford 1974
    —. & Kirk Varnedoe, Christel Hollevoet, and Robert Frank. *Jasper Johns: Writings, Sketchbook Notes, Interviews*, Museum of Modern Art, New York. NY. 2002
Jill Johnston.
    Jasper Johns: Privileged Information, 1996
D. Judd. *Complete Writings, 1959-1975*, Nova Scotia College of Art and Design, Halifax, Canada, 1975
    —. *Complete Writings, 1975-1986*, Van Abbemuseum, Netherlands, 1987
C.G. Jung.
    Memories, Dreams, Reflections, Collins, London, 1967

Max Kozloff.
Jasper Johns, New York, NY, 1969
Rosalind E. Krauss.
Passages in Modern Sculpture, Thames & Hudson, London, 1977
–. & Christopher Knight. "Split decisions: Jasper Johns in retrospect" Artforum, September, 1996
Carolyn Lanchner.
Jasper Johns, Museum of Modern Art, New York, NY, 2010
Lucy Lippard.
From the Center: feminist essays on women's art, Dutton, New York, NY, 1976
Ad Reinhardt, Abrahams, New York, NY, 1981
Brice Marden.
Paintings, Drawings and Prints 1975-1980, ed. Nicholas Serota, Whitechapel Art Gallery, London, 1987
Anna Moszynska.
Abstract Art, Thames & Hudson, London, 1990
Lynda Nead.
Female Nude: Art, Obscenity and Sexuality, Routledge, London, 1992
Terry A. Neff, ed.
A Quiet Revolution: British Sculpture Since 1965, Thames & Hudson, London, 1987
Fred Orton.
Figuring Jasper Johns, Reaktion Books, 1994
–. *Jasper Johns: The Sculptures*, Henry Moore Institute, Leeds, Yorkshire, 1996
Andreas C. Papadakis, ed.
The New Romantics, Art & Design (vol 4 11/12), Academy Group, London, 1988
–. ed. *British and American Art: The Uneasy Dialectic*, Art & Design (vol 3 9/10, Academy Group, London, 1987
–. ed. *Abstract Art and the Rediscovery of the Spiritual*, Art & Design (vol 3 5/6), Academy Group, London, 1987
Debra Pearlman.
Where Is Jasper Johns? (Adventures in Art), Prestel Publishing, 2006
Gaetan Picon.
Surrealists and Surrealism 1919-1939, Skira/ Macmillan, London, 1983
Ad Reinhardt.
Art as Art: The Selected Writings of Ad Reinhardt, University of California Press, Berkeley, CA, 1991
Alain Robbe-Grillet, Jasper Johns, and Ben Stoltzfus.
The Target, 2006
Corrine Robins, ed.
The Pluralist Era: American Art 1968-1981, Harper & Row, New York, NY, 1984
Franz Roh.
German Art in the Twentieth Century: Painting, Sculpture, Architecture, Thames & Hudson, London, 1968
J. Rondeau.
Jasper Johns: Gray, Art Institute of Chicago, 2007
Barbara Rose.

American Art Since, London, 1900, Thames & Hudson, London, 1967

—. "Decoys and Doubles: Jasper Johns and the Modernist Mind", *Arts*, May 1976

—. "Jasper Johns: Pictures and Concepts", *Arts*, November 1977

—. *American Painting*, Skira/Rizzoli International, New York, NY, 1986

—. "Jasper Johns – The Seasons", *Vogue*, January 1987

Harold Rosenberg.

"Jasper Johns: Things the Mind Already Knows," *Vogue*, 1964

Robert Rosenblum.

Modern Painting and the Northern Romantic Tradition, Thames & Hudson, London, 1978

Mark Rosenthal.

Jasper Johns: Work Since 1974, New York, NY, 1989

J. Russell.

"The Seasons: Forceful Paintings from Jasper Johns", *New York Times*, 6 February 1987

Irwin Sandler.

The Triumph of American Painting, Harper & Row 1970

—. *American Art of the 1960s*, Harper & Row, New York, NY, 1988

—. *Art of the Postmodern Era: From the 1960s to the Early 1990s*, HarperCollins, London, 1997

Jean-Paul Sartre.

Being and Nothingness, tr Hazel Barnes, Methuen, London, 1969

P. Schjeldahl.

Art in Our Time: The Saatchi Collection, Lund Humphries, London, 1984

D. Shapiro

Jasper Johns, Drawings, Abrams, New York, NY, 1984

—. & Cecil Shapiro, eds. *Abstract Expressionism: A Critical Record*, Cambridge University Press 1990

Nikos Stangos, ed.

Concepts of Modern Art, Thames & Hudson, London, 1981

Leo Steinberg.

"Jasper Johns: The First Seven Years of His Art", in *Other Criteria: Confront-ations with Twentieth-Century Art*, Oxford University Press, New York 1972

F. Stella.

Working Space, Harvard University Press, Cambridge, MA, 1986

Kristine Stiles & P. Selz, eds.

Theories & Documents of Contemporary Art: A Sourcebook of Artists' Writings, University of California Press, Berkeley, CA, 1996

D. Sylvester.

"Interview", *Jasper Johns Drawings*, Museum of Modern Art, Oxford 1974

—. *About Modern Art*, Chatto & Windus, London, 1996

Maurice Tuchman.

The New York School, Thames & Hudson, London, 1971

—. *The Spiritual in Art: Abstract Painting 1880-1985*, Los Angeles County Museum of Art/ Abbeville Press, New York, NY, 1986

Paul Vogt.

Contemporary Painting, Abrams, New York, NY, 1981

Diane Waldman.

Mark Rothko, Thames & Hudson, London, 1978
P. Webb.
   The Erotic Arts, Secker & Warburg, London, 1983
Daniel Wheeler.
   Art Since Mid-Century: 1945 to the Present, Thames & Hudson, London, 1991
Jeffrey Weiss.
   Jasper Johns: An Allegory of Painting, 1955-1965, Yale University Press, 2007
Gerard Woods *et al*, eds.
   Art Without Boundaries, Thames & Hudson, London, 1972
John Yau. *A Thing Among Things: The Art of Jasper Johns*, Distributed Art
   Publishers, 2008

WEBSITE

jasperjohns.com

THE ART OF
ANDY GOLDSWORTHY

COMPLETE WORKS: SPECIAL EDITION
(PAPERBACK and HARDBACK)

by William Malpas

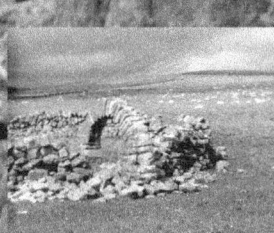 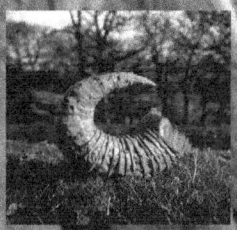

A new, special edition of the study of the contemporary British sculptor, Andy Goldsworthy, including a new introduction, new bibliography and many new illustrations.

This is the most comprehensive, up-to-date, well-researched and in-depth account of Goldsworthy's art available anywhere.

Andy Goldsworthy makes land art. His sculpture is a sensitive, intuitive response to nature, light, time, growth, the seasons and the earth. Goldsworthy's environmental art is becoming ever more popular: 1993's art book *Stone* was a bestseller; the press raved about Goldsworthy taking over a number of London West End art galleries in 1994; during 1995 Goldsworthy designed a set of Royal Mail stamps and had a show at the British Museum. Malpas surveys all of Goldsworthy's art, and analyzes his relation with other land artists such as Robert Smithson, Walter de Maria, Richard Long and David Nash, and his place in the contemporary British art scene.

The Art of Andy Goldsworthy discusses all of Goldsworthy's important and recent exhibitions and books, including the *Sheepfolds* project; the TV documentaries; *Wood* (1996); the New York Holocaust memorial (2003); and Goldsworthy's collaboration on a dance performance.

Illustrations: 70 b/w, 1 colour. 330 pages. New, special, 2nd edition.
Publisher: Crescent Moon Publishing. Distributor: Gardners Books.

ISBN 1-86171-059-3 (9781861710598) (Paperback) £25.00 / $44.00

ISBN 1-86171-080-1 (9781861710802) (Hardback) £60.00 / $105.00

ANDY GOLDSWORTHY
IN CLOSE-UP

SPECIAL EDITION (HARDBACK and PAPERBACK)

by William Malpas

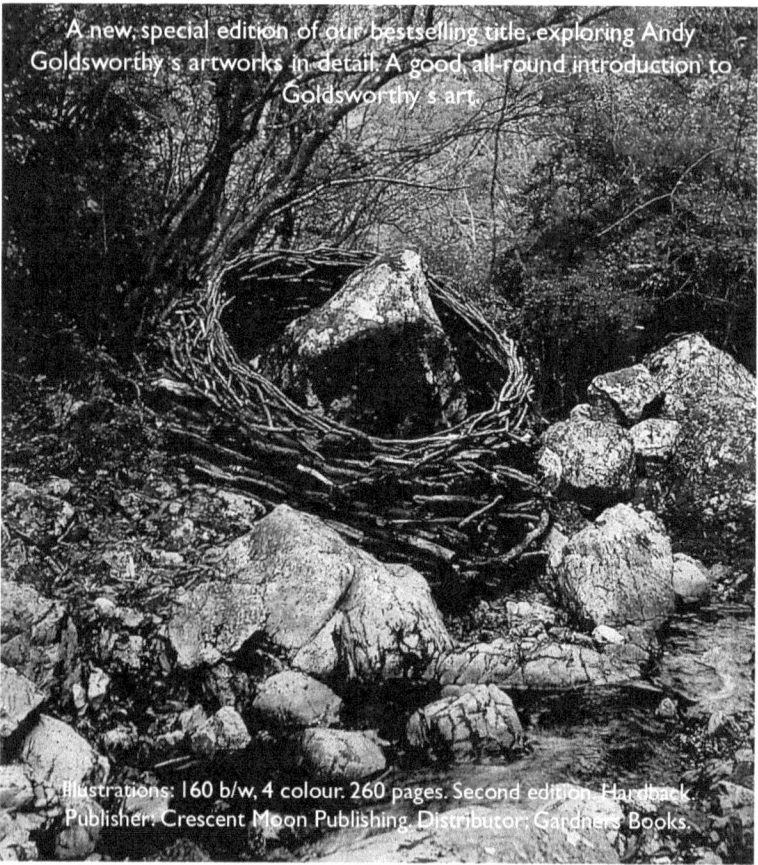

A new, special edition of our bestselling title, exploring Andy Goldsworthy's artworks in detail. A good, all-round introduction to Goldsworthy's art.

Illustrations: 160 b/w, 4 colour. 260 pages. Second edition. Hardback. Publisher: Crescent Moon Publishing. Distributor: Gardners Books.

ISBN 1-86171-094-1 (9781861710949) (Hbk) £60.00 / $105.00

ISBN 1-86171-091-7 (9781861710919) (Pbk) £25.00 / $44.00

Available from bookstores. amazon.com, play.com, tesco.com, and other web-sites.
In the United States from Baker & Taylor, (800) 7753760 or (800) 7751100 or (908) 5417062. electser@btol.com or btinfo@btol.com.

ANDY GOLDSWORTHY

TOUCHING NATURE:
SPECIAL EDITION

(PAPERBACK and HARDBACK)

by William Malpas

A new, special and updated edition of our bestselling title, providing an excellent general introduction to the art of Andy Goldsworthy.

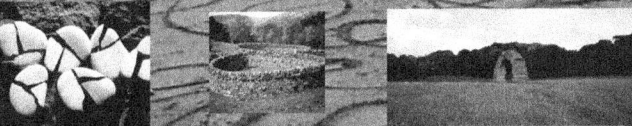

Illustrations: 75 b/w, 2 colour. 354 pages. Third edition. Paperback.

Publisher: Crescent Moon Publishing. Distributor: Gardners Books.

ISBN 1-86171-056-9 (9781861717) (Paperback) £25.00 / $44.00

ISBN 1-86171-087-9 (9781861710871) (Hardback) £60.00 / $105.00

LAND ART

A COMPLETE GUIDE TO LANDSCAPE, ENVIRONMENTAL, EARTHWORKS, NATURE, SCULPTURE AND INSTALLATION ART

by William Malpas

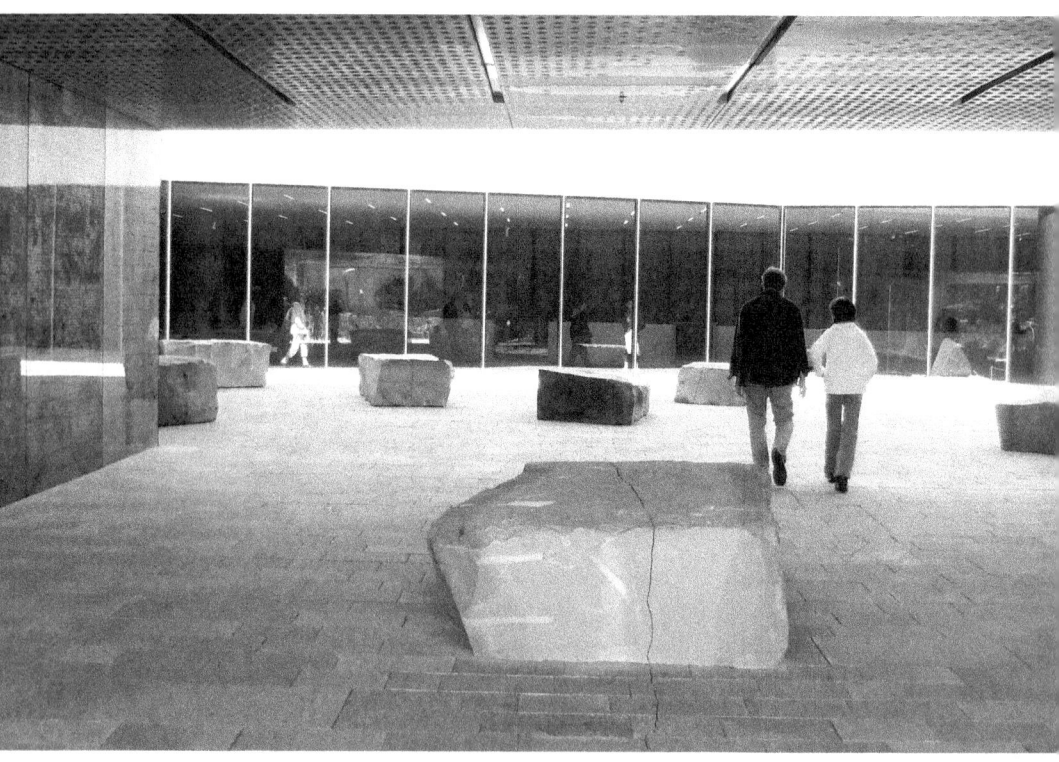

A new, special edition of our popular book on land art.
Chapters on land artists such as Robert Smithson, Walter de Maria, Christo, Michael Heizer, Richard Long and Andy Goldsworthy.

Illustrations: 35 b/w, 2 colour. 314 pages. First edition. Paperback.

Publisher: Crescent Moon Publishing. Distributor: Gardners Books.

ISBN 1-86171-062-3 (9781861710628) £25.00 / $44.00

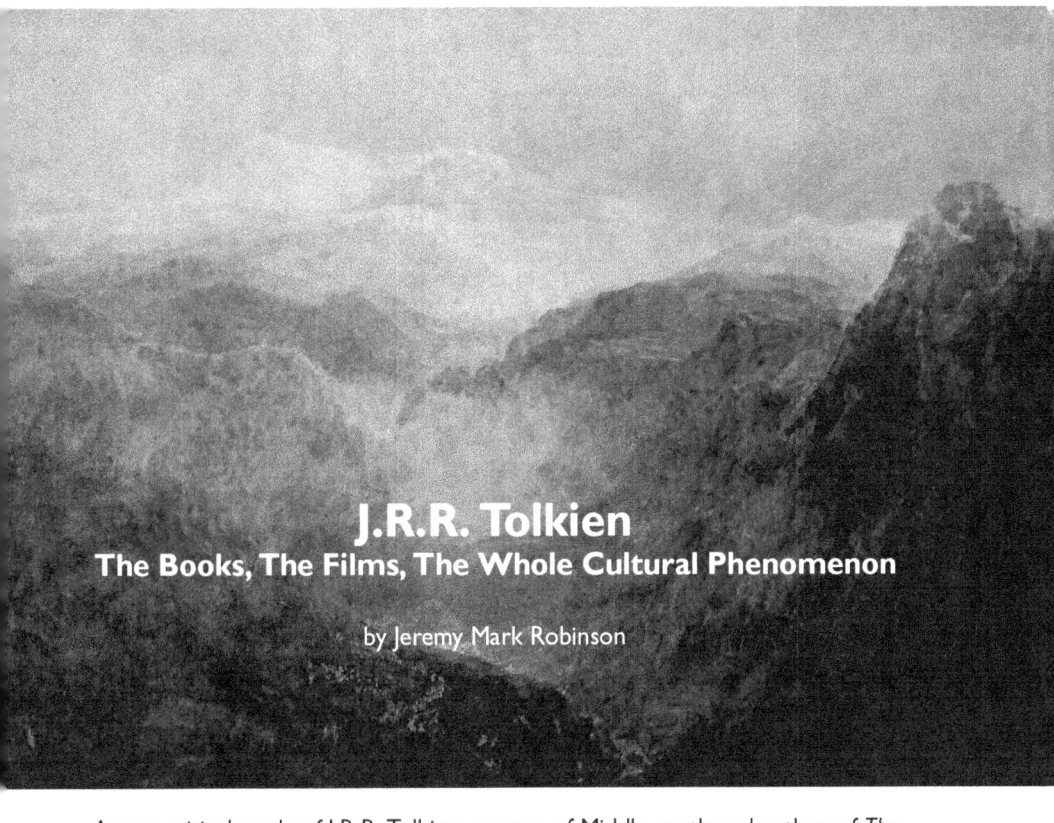

J.R.R. Tolkien
The Books, The Films, The Whole Cultural Phenomenon

by Jeremy Mark Robinson

A new critical study of J.R.R. Tolkien, creator of Middle-earth and author of *The Lord of the Rings, The Hobbit* and *The Silmarillion*, among other books.
This new critical study explores Tolkien's major writings (*The Lord of the Rings, The Hobbit, Beowulf: The Monster and the Critics, The Letters, The Silmarillion* and *The History of Middle-earth* volumes); Tolkien and fairy tales; the mythological, political and religious aspects of Tolkien's Middle-earth; the critics' response to Tolkien's fiction over the decades; the Tolkien industry (merchandizing, toys, role-playing games, posters, Tolkien societies, conferences and the like); Tolkien in visual and fantasy art; the cultural aspects of The Lord of the Rings (from the 1950s to the present); Tolkien's fiction's relationship with other fantasy fiction, such as C.S. Lewis and *Harry Potter*; and the TV, radio and film versions of Tolkien's books, including the 2001-03 Hollywood interpretations of *The Lord of the Rings*.
This new book draws on contemporary cultural theory and analysis and offers a sympathetic and illuminating (and sceptical) account of the Tolkien phenomenon. This book is designed to appeal to the general reader (and viewer) of Tolkien: it is written in a clear, jargon-free and easily-accessible style.

754pp ISBN 1-86171-057-7 £25.00 / $37.50

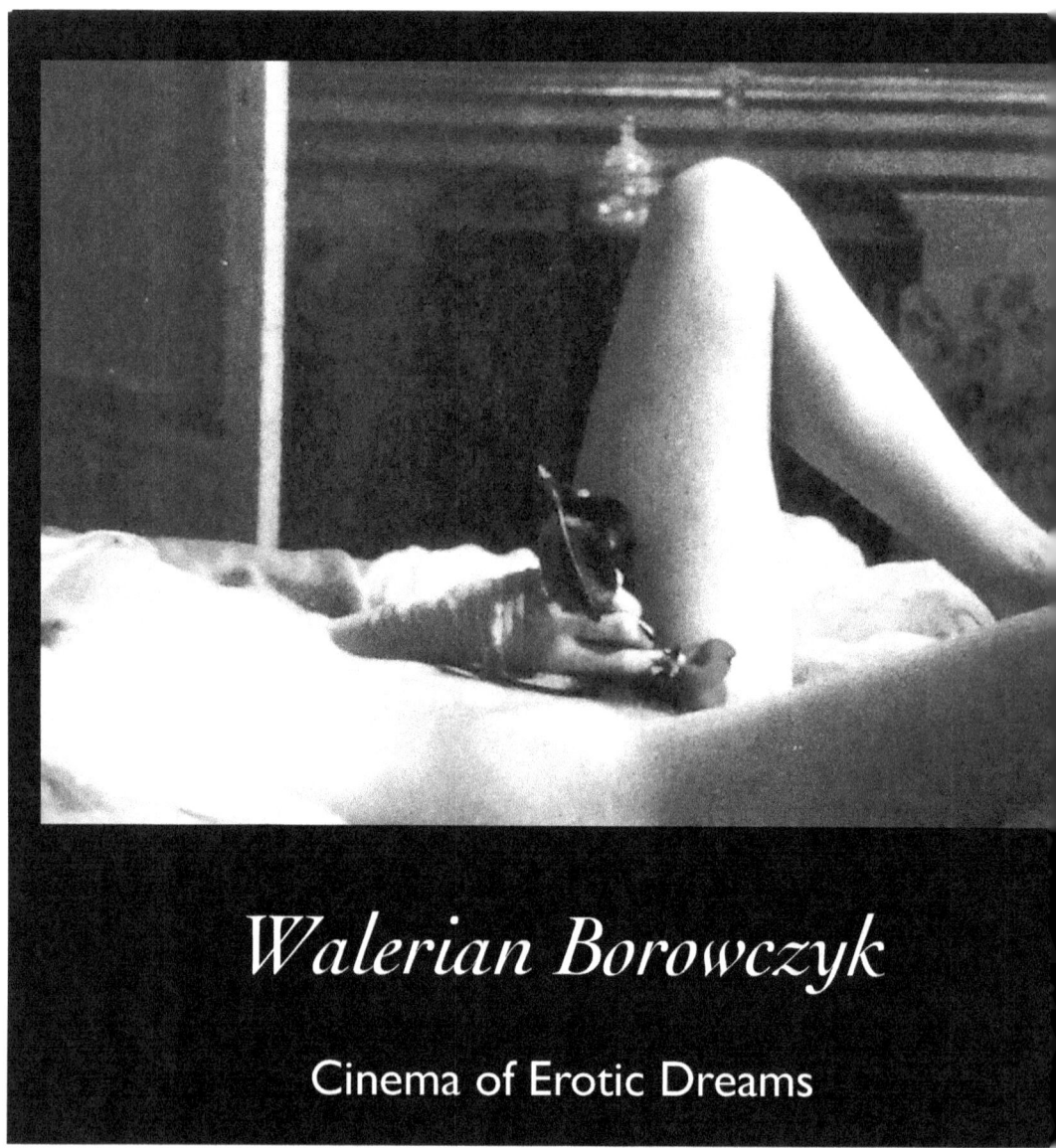

Walerian Borowczyk

Cinema of Erotic Dreams

by Jeremy Mark Robinson

Walerian Borowczyk (1923-2006) was a Polish artist, animator and filmmaker who lived in France for much of his life. He is the author of European art cinema masterpieces Goto: Island of Love, Blanche and Immoral Tales, some surreal animated shorts, and controversial films such as The Beast. This new book concentrates on Borowczyk's feature films, from Goto to Love Rites, which contain some of the most extraordinary images and scenes in recent cinema. Erotica for some, porn for others, Borowczyk's films are highly idiosyncratic and unforgettable.

Bibliography, notes, illustrations   240pp.
Paperback   ISBN 9781861712301   £15.00 / $30.00

Jean-Luc Godard

The Passion of Cinema /
Le Passion de Cinéma

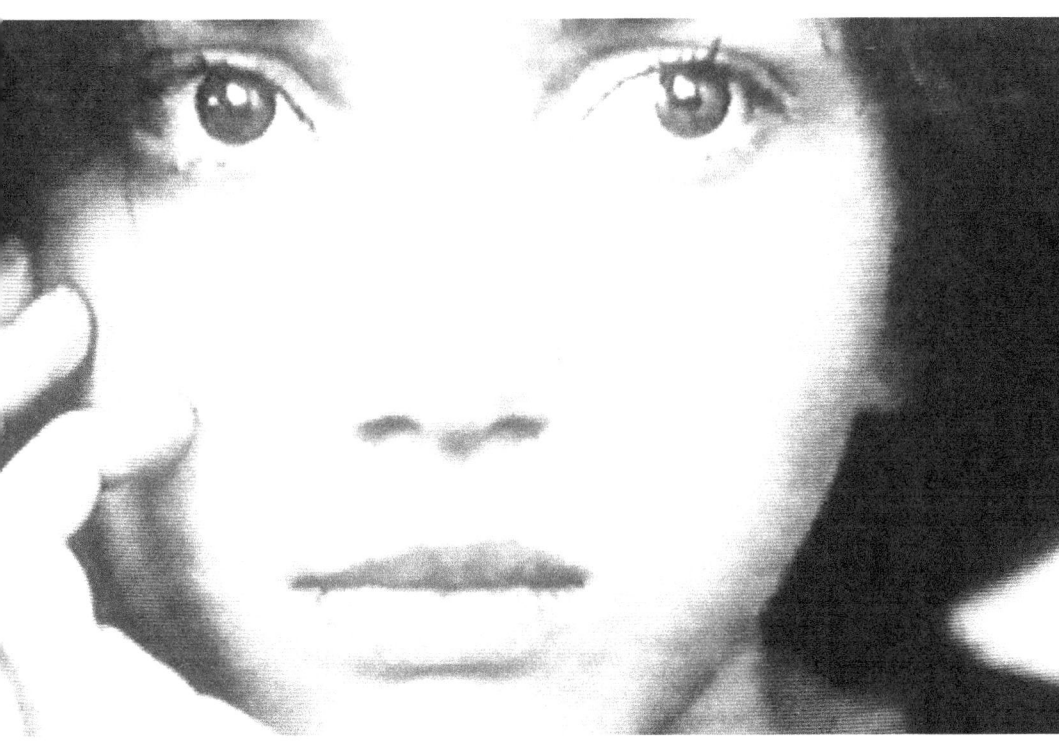

by Jeremy Mark Robinson

A new study of the French filmmaker Jean-Luc Godard (b. 1930),
director of iconic films such as *Breathless, Weekend, Pierrot le Fou,
Passion* and *Vivre Sa vie*. This book explores 27 of Godard's major films,
from *Breathless* to *Notre Musique*, and includes a scene by scene
analysis of Godard's controversial 1985 movie of the Virgin Mary,
Je Vous Salue, Marie.

Bibliography, notes, illustrations   420pp
Hardback   ISBN 9781761712271   £50.00 / $100.00

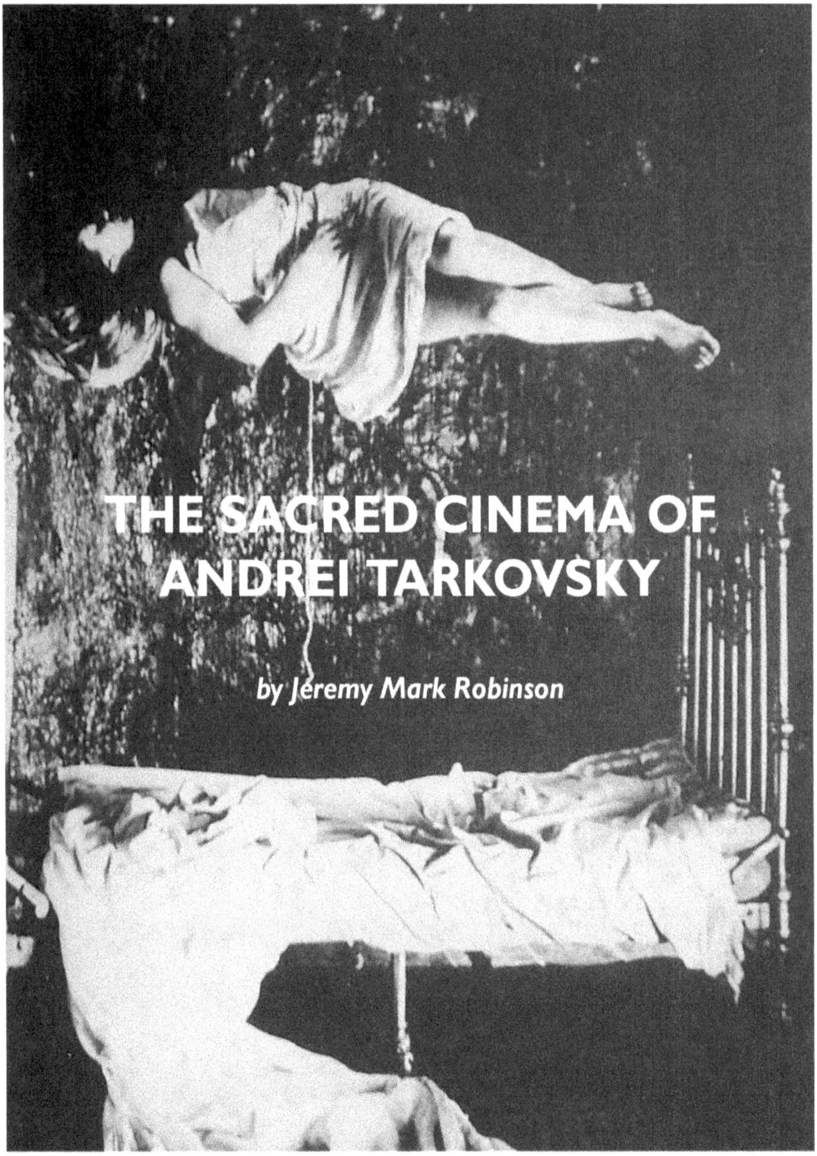

THE SACRED CINEMA OF ANDREI TARKOVSKY

by Jeremy Mark Robinson

A new study of the Russian filmmaker Andrei Tarkovsky (1932-1986), director of seven feature films, including *Andrei Roublyov, Mirror, Solaris, Stalker* and *The Sacrifice*.

This is one of the most comprehensive and detailed studies of Tarkovsky's cinema available. Every film is explored in depth, with scene-by-scene analyses. All aspects of Tarkovsky's output are critiqued, including editing, camera, staging, script, budget, collaborations, production, sound, music, performance and spirituality. Tarkovsky is placed with a European New Wave tradition of filmmaking, alongside directors like Ingmar Bergman, Carl Theodor Dreyer, Pier Paolo Pasolini and Robert Bresson.

An essential addition to film studies.

Illustrations: 150 b/w, 4 colour. 682 pages. First edition. Hardback.

Publisher: Crescent Moon Publishing. Distributor: Gardners Books.

ISBN 1-86171-096-8 (9781861710963) £60.00 / $105.00

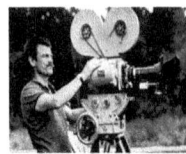

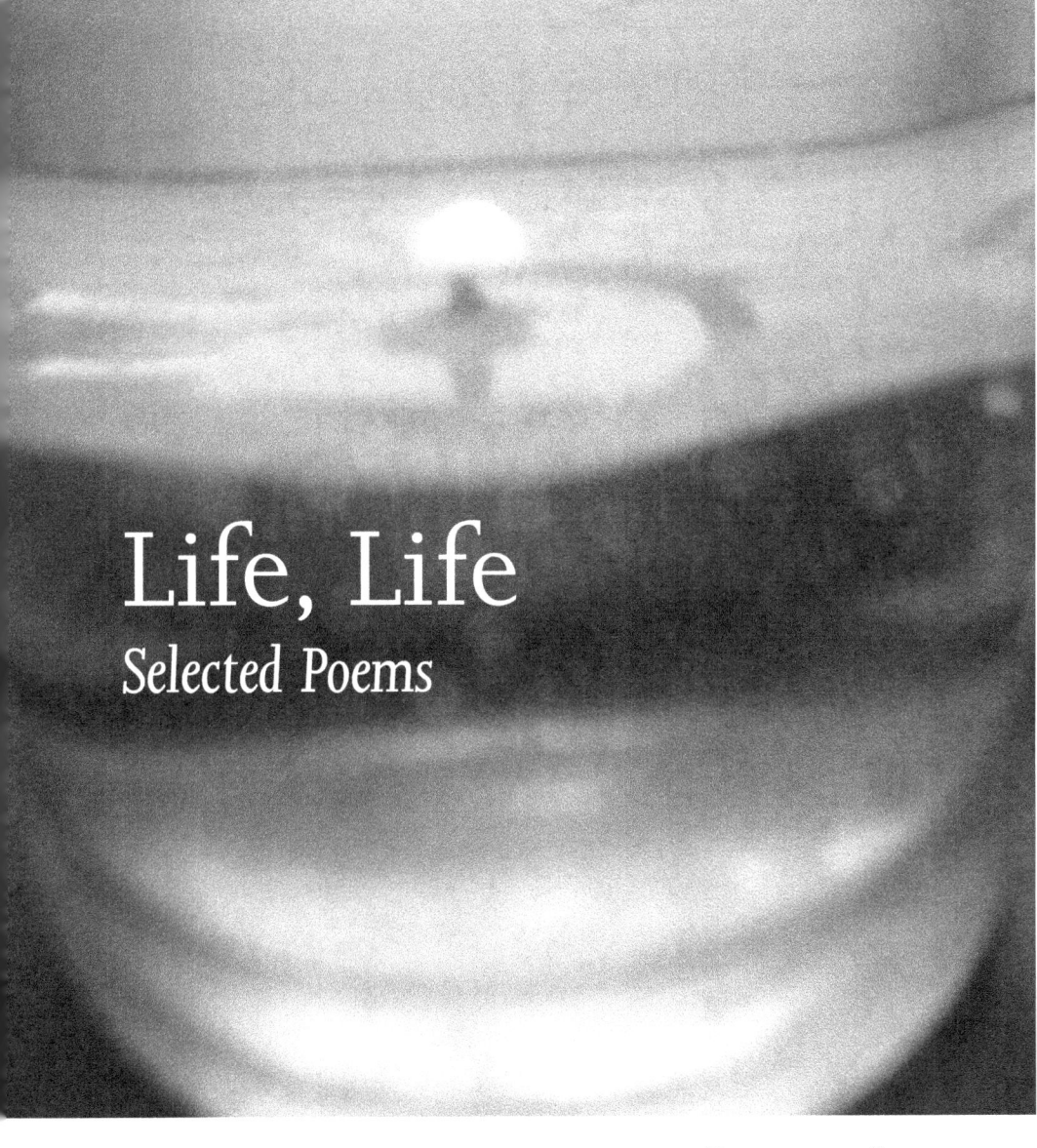

Life, Life
Selected Poems

Arseny Tarkovsky

translated and edited by Virginia Rounding

Arseny Tarkovsky is the neglected Russian poet, father of the acclaimed film director
Andrei Tarkovsky. This new book gathers together many of Tarkovsky's most lyrical
and heartfelt poems, in Rounding's clear, new translations. Many of Tarkovsky's poems
appeared in his son's films, such as *Mirror, Stalker, Nostalghia* and *The Sacrifice*.
There is an introduction by Rounding, and a bibliography of both Arseny and Andrei Tarkovsky.

Bibliography and notes   110pp   2nd ed   ISBN 1-86171-114-X   £10.00 / $20.00

In the Dim Void

Samuel Beckett's Late Trilogy:
Company, Ill Seen, Ill Said and *Worstward Ho*

by Gregory Johns

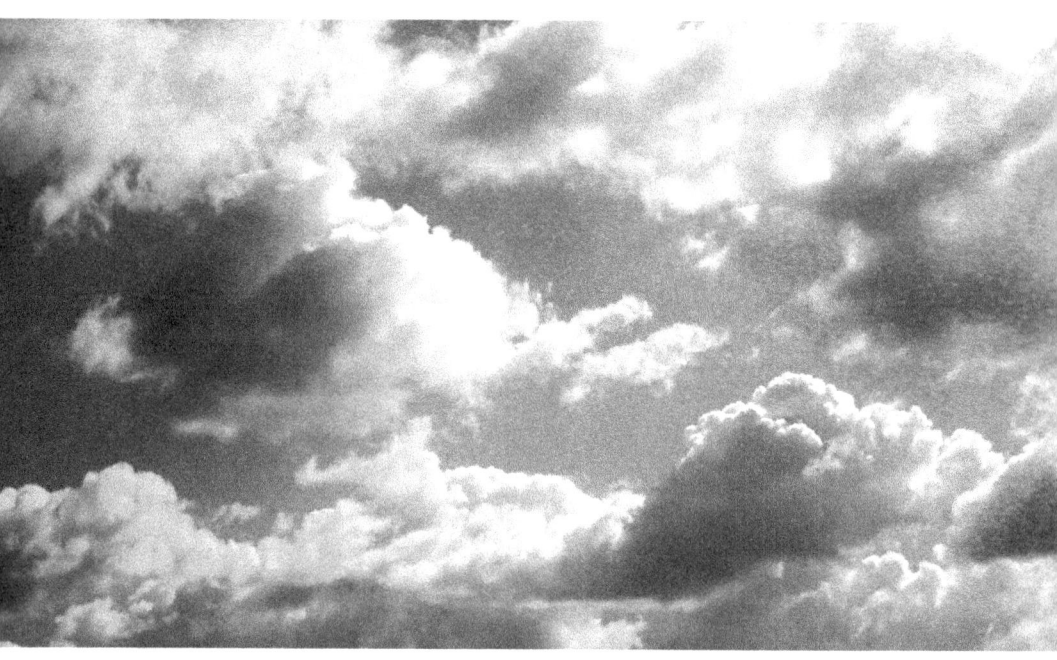

This book discusses the luminous beauty and dense, rigorous poetry of Beckett's late works, *Company, Ill Seen, Ill Said* and *Worstward Ho*. Johns looks back over Beckett's long writing career, charting the development from the *Molloy-Malone Dies-Unnamable* trilogy through the 'fizzles' of the 1960s to the elegiac lyricism of the *Company* series. Johns compares the trilogy with late plays such as *Ghosts, Footfalls* and *Rockaby*.

Bibliography, notes. 120pp
ISBN 1861710712 and ISBN 1861712356   £10.00 / $20.00

CRESCENT MOON PUBLISHING

ARTS, PAINTING, SCULPTURE

The Art of Andy Goldsworthy: Complete Works
Andy Goldsworthy: Touching Nature
Andy Goldsworthy in Close-Up
Andy Goldsworthy: Pocket Guide
Andy Goldsworthy In America
Land Art: A Complete Guide
Richard Long: The Art of Walking
The Art of Richard Long: Complete Works
Richard Long in Close-Up
Richard Long: Pocket Guide
Land Art In the UK
Land Art in Close-Up
Land Art In the U.S.A.
Land Art: Pocket Guide
Installation Art in Close-Up
Minimal Art and Artists In the 1960s and After
Colourfield Painting
Land Art DVD, TV documentary
Andy Goldsworthy DVD, TV documentary
The Erotic Object: Sexuality in Sculpture From Prehistory to the Present Day
Sex in Art: Pornography and Pleasure in Painting and Sculpture
Postwar Art
Sacred Gardens: The Garden in Myth, Religion and Art
Glorification: Religious Abstraction in Renaissance and 20th Century Art
Early Netherlandish Painting
Leonardo da Vinci
Piero della Francesca
Giovanni Bellini
Fra Angelico: Art and Religion in the Renaissance
Mark Rothko: The Art of Transcendence
Frank Stella: American Abstract Artist
Jasper Johns: Painting By Numbers
Brice Marden
Alison Wilding: The Embrace of Sculpture
Vincent van Gogh: Visionary Landscapes
Eric Gill: Nuptials of God
Constantin Brancusi: Sculpting the Essence of Things
Max Beckmann
Caravaggio
Gustave Moreau
Egon Schiele: Sex and Death In Purple Stockings
Delizioso Fotografico Fervore: Works In Process 1
Sacro Cuore: Works In Process 2
The Light Eternal: J.M.W. Turner
The Madonna Glorified: Karen Arthurs

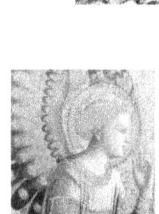
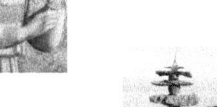
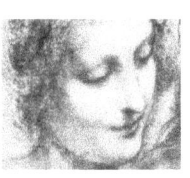
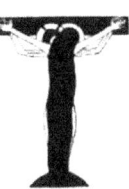
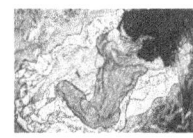

LITERATURE

J.R.R. Tolkien: The Books, The Films, The Whole Cultural Phenomenon
J.R.R. Tolkien: Pocket Guide
Tolkien's Heroic Quest
The *Earthsea* Books of Ursula Le Guin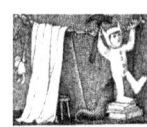
Beauties, Beasts and Enchantment: Classic French Fairy Tales
Sexing Hardy: Thomas Hardy and Feminism
Thomas Hardy's *Tess of the d'Urbervilles*
Thomas Hardy's *Jude the Obscure*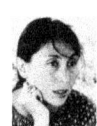
Thomas Hardy: The Tragic Novels
Love and Tragedy: Thomas Hardy
The Poetry of Landscape in Hardy
Wessex Revisited: Thomas Hardy and John Cowper Powys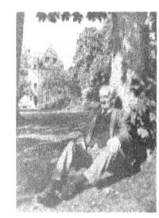
Wolfgang Iser: Essays and Interviews
Petrarch, Dante and the Troubadours
Maurice Sendak and the Art of Children's Book Illustration
Andrea Dworkin
Cixous, Irigaray, Kristeva: The *Jouissance* of French Feminism
Julia Kristeva: Art, Love, Melancholy, Philosophy, Semiotics and Psychoanalysis
Hélène Cixous I Love You: The *Jouissance* of Writing
Luce Irigaray: Lips, Kissing, and the Politics of Sexual Difference
Peter Redgrove: Here Comes the Flood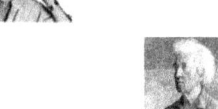
Peter Redgrove: Sex-Magic-Poetry-Cornwall
Lawrence Durrell: Between Love and Death, East and West
Love, Culture & Poetry: Lawrence Durrell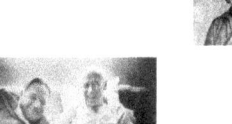
Cavafy: Anatomy of a Soul
German Romantic Poetry: Goethe, Novalis, Heine, Hölderlin
Feminism and Shakespeare
Shakespeare: Love, Poetry & Magic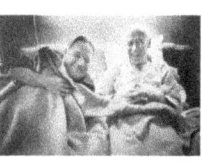
The Passion of D.H. Lawrence
D.H. Lawrence: Symbolic Landscapes
D.H. Lawrence: Infinite Sensual Violence
Rimbaud: Arthur Rimbaud and the Magic of Poetry
The Ecstasies of John Cowper Powys
Sensualism and Mythology: The Wessex Novels of John Cowper Powys
Amorous Life: John Cowper Powys and the Manifestation of Affectivity (H.W. Fawkner)
Postmodern Powys: New Essays on John Cowper Powys (Joe Boulter)
Rethinking Powys: Critical Essays on John Cowper Powys
Paul Bowles & Bernardo Bertolucci
Rainer Maria Rilke
Joseph Conrad: *Heart of Darkness*
In the Dim Void: Samuel Beckett
Samuel Beckett Goes into the Silence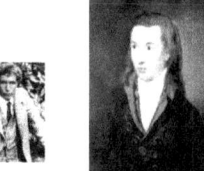
André Gide: Fiction and Fervour
Jackie Collins and the Blockbuster Novel
Blinded By Her Light: The Love-Poetry of Robert Graves
The Passion of Colours: Travels In Mediterranean Lands
Poetic Forms

MEDIA, CINEMA, FEMINISM and CULTURAL STUDIES

J.R.R. Tolkien: The Books, The Films, The Whole Cultural Phenomenon
J.R.R. Tolkien: Pocket Guide
The *Lord of the Rings* Movies: Pocket Guide
The Ghost Dance: The Origins of Religion
Cixous, Irigaray, Kristeva: The *Jouissance* of French Feminism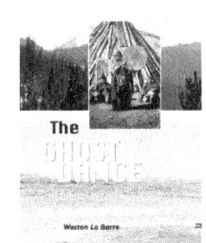
Julia Kristeva: Art, Love, Melancholy, Philosophy, Semiotics and Psychoanalysis
Luce Irigaray: Lips, Kissing, and the Politics of Sexual Difference
Hélene Cixous I Love You: The *Jouissance* of Writing
Andrea Dworkin
'Cosmo Woman': The World of Women's Magazines
Women in Pop Music
Discovering the Goddess (Geoffrey Ashe)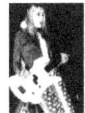
The Poetry of Cinema
The Sacred Cinema of Andrei Tarkovsky
Andrei Tarkovsky: Pocket Guide
Andrei Tarkovsky: *Mirror*: Pocket Movie Guide
Andrei Tarkovsky: *The Sacrifice*: Pocket Movie Guide
Walerian Borowczyk: Cinema of Erotic Dreams
Jean-Luc Godard: The Passion of Cinema
John Hughes and Eighties Cinema
Ferris Bueller's Day Off: Pocket Movie Guide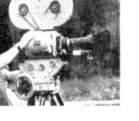
Jean-Luc Godard: Pocket Guide
The Cinema of Richard Linklater
Liv Tyler: Star In Ascendance
Blade Runner and the Films of Philip K. Dick
Paul Bowles and Bernardo Bertolucci
Media Hell: Radio, TV and the Press
An Open Letter to the BBC
Detonation Britain: Nuclear War in the UK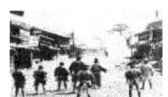
Feminism and Shakespeare
Wild Zones: Pornography, Art and Feminism
Sex in Art: Pornography and Pleasure in Painting and Sculpture
Sexing Hardy: Thomas Hardy and Feminism

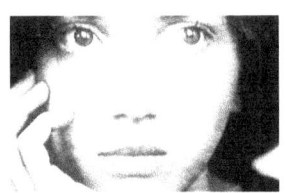

In my view *The Light Eternal* is among the very best of all the material I read on Turner. (Douglas Graham, director of the Turner Museum, Denver, Colorado)

The Light Eternal is a model monograph, an exemplary job. The subject matter of the book is beautifully organised and dead on beam. (Lawrence Durrell)

It is amazing for me to see my work treated with such passion and respect. (Andrea Dworkin)

Sex-Magic-Poetry-Cornwall is a very rich essay... It is like a brightly-lighted box. (Peter Redgrove)

CRESCENT MOON PUBLISHING
P.O. Box 393, Maidstone, Kent, ME14 5XU, United Kingdom. www.crmoon.com

www.ingramcontent.com/pod-product-compliance
Lightning Source LLC
Chambersburg PA
CBHW051330220526
45468CB00004B/1580